THE LIBRANOS

What the media won't tell you about
Justin Trudeau's corruption

EZRA LEVANT

TABLE OF CONTENTS

ACKNOWLEDGEMENTS

Thank you to the team of reporters at Rebel News who have done more accountability journalism about Trudeau than most other media organizations ten times our size — and all without a dime of public money. This book relies in part on their research, and I'm grateful for their support. The fact that Trudeau and his cronies obsessively defame us, censor us and try to deplatform us is proof that we're speaking truth to power. Thanks to our whole team for your courage.

INTRODUCTION

Justin Trudeau's term as prime minister has been a disaster, but you wouldn't know it if your only source of news was the Media Party — the liberal-leaning clique of reporters and commentators who would rather take a selfie with Trudeau than ask him a tough question.

It's gotten even worse as the few remaining independent newspapers in Canada signed up for Trudeau's $600 million media bail-out. You just can't trust the media anymore, and Canadians know it.

Trudeau wasn't properly vetted by the media in 2015. He slouched across the finish line on the strength of his last name and Baby Boomer nostalgia for the Trudeaumania of the 1960s. The result has been an incompetent government that has hurt Canada's prosperity at home and our relationships abroad.

Canadians know something is desperately wrong — the latest polls show 63% of voters disapprove of Trudeau's leadership. But with a full-court press from the Liberal Party, the Media Party and hundreds of third-party campaign groups (including some funded by the same Media Party journalists who will report on the 2019 election) there's a good chance Trudeau will be re-elected, even if it's with just a minority.

That's what this book is about: it's really the case against Justin Trudeau. But it's not about any one policy or gaffe. It's about the real risk of Trudeau: the culture of corruption and cronyism that he has brought with him, that's corroding our democracy and even our rule of law.

The Libranos is the story of grifters and scammers and secret favours for friends. It's about sociopaths who don't hesitate for a second to break the law if it gets them ahead. But mainly it's about an unaccomplished man who has nothing to offer but a famous last name and nice hair — and how he took power anyway, and might just do it again.

CHAPTER 1

WHAT'S A LIBRANO?

When Justin Trudeau was elected prime minister on the night of October 19, 2015, few could have imagined that he would end up leading what is arguably the most unethical, corrupt, even criminal governments in modern Canadian history. On the contrary, Trudeau had promised to make Canada's federal government more accountable, more transparent, more democratic and more answerable to those who are supposed to be its bosses, the citizens of Canada. As he appeared on stage that night at Liberal headquarters in Montreal, Trudeau made a promise to those people. "I know that I am on stage tonight for one reason and one reason only: because you put me here. And you gave me clear marching orders," *he said.*[1] "You want a prime minister who knows that if Canadians are to trust their government, their government needs to trust Canadians, a PM who understands that openness and transparency means better, smarter decisions."

Trudeau was of course pompously contrasting himself with what he accused his predecessor, Conservative Prime Minister Stephen Harper,

---

1   "Justin Trudeau, for the record: 'We beat fear with hope'," *Maclean's,* Oct. 20, 2015, *https://www.macleans.ca/politics/ottawa/justin-trudeau-for-the-record-we-beat-fear-with-hope/.*

of being. Trudeau had built his entire leadership of the party, since he ran to take over the Liberals in 2013, on being the *"anti-Harper."* The Harper Conservatives certainly had offered the Liberal Party some ammunition to accuse them of lapses in democratic accountability. The Tories didn't help their reputation with their scandals involving Senate appointments, misbehaving MPs, and the occasional attempts to cover up embarrassing screwups. When a party is in power for nine years, as the Tories were, you have to expect that a certain amount of blight will grow on it. However, that's a lot less common after only four years in power.

"The Conservatives have forgotten about the value of service," *Trudeau charged* in his speech accepting the Liberal leadership after his victory in 2013.[2] "Mr. Harper is showing us how governments grow out of touch."

The Liberals under Trudeau had somehow magically recast themselves as the ethical party, the responsible party, the accountable party, the transparent party. And they did it in less than a decade after Harper had been elected as a direct response to the Liberals' deep-rooted corruption and criminality. Canadians sure do have short memories sometimes.

If the title of this book sounds familiar, that's because it was first popularized just over 15 years ago, when the *Western Standard*, the now defunct Calgary-based magazine that I founded, printed a cover story called "The Libranos" (with the 's' stylized as a dollar sign), in response to the hail of corruption and criminal charges that were coming down on the then Liberal government and its cronies. The term, which had first been dreamt up by blogger Kate McMillan (her blog is called Small Dead Animals), was a take-off on the then wildly popular *Sopranos* TV series on HBO, which was a tale about a fictional New Jersey mafia crime family. Our cover had satirized the famous black, grey and red promotional posters for the TV show by replacing

---

2   "Full text: Justin Trudeau's speech for the Liberal leadership showcase," The Globe and Mail, April 6, 2013, *https://www.theglobeandmail.com/news/politics/full-text-justin-trudeaus-speech-for-the-liberal-leadership-showcase/article10827923/.*

the HBO mobsters with top Liberals, including former prime minister Jean Chrétien, then prime minister Paul Martin, and several others.

(That would include the wonderfully named Alfonse Gagliano, a longtime Liberal cabinet minister whose name kept appearing in news stories about backroom deals. As an added bonus, he looked like he was sent up from Central Casting's mob-movie department, and he just happens to have faced more than one allegation over the years of *literally being connected* to notorious *mafia types*.[3, 4] Gagliano, an accountant who immigrated to Canada from Sicily, has always denied any links to organized crime. He claims that his political career *was ended* by prejudice against Italians.[5] The Liberal government tried to make him ambassador to the Vatican — *the Vatican rejected him* — and then, ambassador to Denmark, until they finally *removed him* when his links to scandal came to light.[6 7])

There was good reason for the satirical comparison with the mafia: The Liberal government elected under Jean Chrétien in 1993 had racked up a long list of scandals over its decade of power, but nothing had been seen in Canada in modern history that reached the scale of criminality of the sponsorship corruption scandal, or as it came to be known, Adscam.

3   Greg B. Smith, "Stoolie: Canada pol in mob," *New York Daily News*, Nov. 8, 2004, *https://www.nydailynews.com/archives/news/stoolie-canada-pol-mob-article-1.637030.*

4   "Gagliano denies ties to crime family," CBC News, Nov. 18, 2004, *https://www.cbc.ca/news/canada/gagliano-denies-ties-to-crime-family-1.510138.*

5   "Volpe victim of racism," *Victoria Times-Colonist*, Sept. 26, 2006, *https://web.archive.org/web/20151109044808/ http://www.canada.com/victoriatimescolonist/news/canada/story.html?id=22e1443e-6040-4440-8ca2-7404e896d62a.*

6   Daniel Leblanc, "Vatican shuts out Gagliano," *The Globe and Mail,* June 11, 2003, *https://www.theglobeandmail.com/news/national/vatican-shuts-out-gagliano/article25285820/.*

7   "Ambassador Gagliano fired as critical report released," CBC News, Feb. 10, 2004, *https://www.cbc.ca/news/canada/ambassador-gagliano-fired-as-critical-report-released-1.514411.*

After the Chrétien Liberals had set up a juicy federal fund to buy ads, and promote publicity, boosting Canadian federalism in order to counter the separatist movement in Quebec, the party then proceeded to funnel millions of dollars to their friends, cronies and, of course, the party itself. A subsequent investigation would reveal stories of cash-stuffed envelopes being passed between Liberal operatives in dark restaurants, along with fake invoices and secret code names. And the entire affair was run with the help of corrupt government ministers. Several Liberals were sent to jail. It was as shocking and vulgar a scandal as Canada has ever seen, the textbook definition of naked corruption: The Liberals were using Canada as their personal piggybank to enrich themselves — one senior Quebec lieutenant for the party, *Jacques Corriveau*, squeezed an astonishing $9 million in fees out of the sponsorship fund[8]. They did it to enrich themselves, but also to tighten their own hold on power, running their political machinery on stolen funds. The Liberals were able to hang on to power as long as they did at least in part using ill-gotten gains to beat the Conservatives. It was a hideous assault on democracy and the public trust.

When the rot had finally set in beyond even the Liberals' ability to hang on, and the party had been weakened by an internal power struggle between Chrétien and his finance minister, Paul Martin, voters finally elected a new government in 2006. Stephen Harper was sent to Ottawa to clean out the fetid government stables that the Liberals had so fouled. Canadians assumed the Liberals had learned their lesson. That their days of corruption were done. That the crime-family governing style of the Libranos was gone for good.

Boy, were they ever wrong.

The Liberals had wanted desperately to make people believe that they were no longer the party of fraud, bribery and graft after the Chrétien years, of course. But no matter who they elected leader, the party couldn't get Canadians to trust them with another government. Paul Martin couldn't do it. Stéphane Dion couldn't do it. Michael Ignatieff definitely couldn't do it. But Justin Trudeau was of a different

---

8   "At the centre of the storm: Jacques Corriveau," CBC News, April 15, 2005, *https://www.cbc.ca/news2/background/groupaction/corriveau_testimony.html.*

generation. Unlike Martin and Dion, he hadn't been in government during those scandalous years of corruption. He was out enjoying his trust-fund lifestyle, taking some university courses off and on or picking up teaching gigs between snowboarding trips. Making him leader would finally rebrand the Liberal as fresh, young and clean. How could anyone think that the youthful and hip Justin Trudeau was part of the old, bloated depraved Liberal political machinery?

But of course he was. In fact, he was the worst of all.

Really, anyone who stopped to think about it for a moment would have realized that Trudeau is the very definition of the arrogant entitlement culture that has long characterized the Liberal Party of Canada. As a Trudeau, his primary asset was merely being heir to the name of his father Pierre, the former prime minister, and a Liberal god. When Trudeau made his public debut giving a eulogy at his father's funeral, Claude Ryan, the former leader of the Quebec Liberal party, said it was "perhaps ... the first manifestation of a dynasty."[9]

Trudeau is the embodiment of the party's incestuous mob-style insularity and self-serving tribal instinct. The man the Liberals sold as the exciting new face of a reborn party was quite the opposite: the epitome of its deeply embedded elitist crony culture run amok. He wasn't just a trust-fund millionaire. He was a trust-fund millionaire who had been raised in the company of all the greasy bagmen, operators, rent-seekers and other party hangers-on that had been the Liberal family since his father was prime minister. This young breath of fresh air supposedly unsullied by grimy party machinations had in fact had been involved with the Liberal party since he was a kid and had even chaired a Liberal task force on renewing the party's youth vote after the 2006 election.[10] This supposed fresh-faced newcomer purportedly untainted by the filth of the Chrétien years had in fact *co-hosted a farewell event for Chrétien* when the then prime minister retired

9   Tonda MacCharles, "Spotlight on Justin sparks talk of dynasty," *Toronto Star*, October 5, 2000.

10   Juliet O'Neill, "Justin Trudeau to spearhead youth renewal of Liberal party," *National Post*, April 7, 2006.

in 2003.[11] Few would have expected it then, but Chrétien, the original Libranos boss, was being toasted by the man who would become the next Libranos boss.

Only, Trudeau would take the Libranos to a whole new level of corruption.

It took the last Liberal government ten years before it had collapsed in the Adscam corruption scandal. In just four years, Trudeau has outdone it handily. There have been scandals that involve taking payoffs, sexual misconduct and, worst of all, corrupting the criminal justice system to help friends and punish his perceived enemies. And so often, Trudeau's misdeeds have roots that run deep into the same underhanded party history built by his father and by Chrétien. The favouritism for SNC-Lavalin; the free trips to the private island of a friend of his father (who also happens to seek government favours); the backroom attempts to rig procurement contracts for Liberal-friendly shipbuilders; making judges out of Liberal friends — these all have the same old noxious Liberal odour. They are all just longtime branches of the Librano family business.

In four short years, Justin Trudeau and his inner circle have brought the Libranos back with a vengeance. They're consolidating even more power than Chrétien did, in the bureaucracy, federal programming and the justice system. Imagine how much stronger they'll become with four more years in power. If they're not thrown out of Ottawa now, they may never be.

---

11   "Chrétien bids adieu to a lifetime in politics," CBC News, Nov. 14, 2003, *https://www.cbc.ca/news/canada/chrtien-bids-adieu-to-a-lifetime-in-politics-1.390751.*

CHAPTER 2

THE LIES TRUDEAU TELLS

"Harper has turned Ottawa into a partisan swamp promoting partisan interests at the expense of public trust," Justin Trudeau thundered during the 2015 election.[12] "We will clean up his mess." He promised an end to patronage appointments. He promised greater transparency. He even promised more free votes for MPs. "For Parliament to work best, its members must be free to do what they have been elected to do — represent their communities in Parliament and hold the government to account."

Trudeau and his pals must have been having a quite a chuckle at the suckers who believed that.

Trudeau, after all, was coming to Ottawa with a mission. The Liberals and their cronies had been cut off from access to the power, the influence, the favours, the perks and the money of government for nine long years of Conservative rule. This scion of their hero, Pierre

---

12   "Trudeau promises more transparent government and changes to the Senate," *The Globe and Mail*, Aug. 11, 2015, *https://www.theglobeandmail.com/ news/politics/trudeau-promises-more-transparent-government-and-changes-to-the-senate/ article25924259/*.

Trudeau, was being sent to get it all back. Patronage wasn't something to be done away with; it was something to control. Patronage was the prize. The entire Liberal family business had long been about doling out power and pork to party friends. And you can't run a business like that with transparency, accountability and free votes.

Trudeau's promises about cleaner government have been shredded one by one. You can't run a clean and transparent government, after all, if your bigger goal is to revive the Liberals' longtime corruption and patronage machine.

Trudeau had said he would make his office and the rest of government more open to Access to Information requests. He not only broke that promise, [13] he brazenly made it even harder for citizens and journalists to get information from his government. He didn't just lie when he promised to make all government open to access to information, including the prime minister and his office — they would still be off limits. But now, the head of a government institution could decline Access to Information requests if they were merely for a "large number of records" and would interfere with government operations. That's a pretty handy excuse to help keep documents under seal for pretty much anything.

In one of his signature promises, and most blatant lies, he vowed to fans of electoral reform that he would put an end to the first-past-the-post voting system in federal politics. "We'll make sure that Canadians have a stronger voice in Ottawa — a voice that reflects and represents them," Trudeau promised in his election campaign. [14] He would make "every vote count" by "ensuring that 2015 will be the last federal election conducted under the first-past-the-post voting system" and move instead toward some form of proportional representation or

---

13 Laura Stone, "Trudeau government breaks campaign promise on access-to-information law," *The Globe and Mail*, June 19, 2017, *https://www.theglobeandmail.com/news/politics/coming-liberal-bills-to-reform-access-to-information-national-security-measures/article35355974/.*

14 Rosemary Barton, "Justin Trudeau vows to end 1st-past-the-post voting in platform speech," CBC News, June 16, 2015, *https://www.cbc.ca/news/politics/justin-trudeau-vows-to-end-1st-past-the-post-voting-in-platform-speech-1.3114902.*

ranked-ballot system. Then he proceeded to perform one of the most audacious farces in political memory: After going through the act of striking a committee to review the alternatives to first-past-the-post, holding town halls with citizens across the country, and even taking a national survey, Trudeau just … killed it.

Of course he did. Because Trudeau wasn't interested in actual electoral reform because of claims it would improve democratic representation. What he was interested in was electoral reform that would tighten the Liberals' hold on power by tilting the system in their favour. What he wanted was a ranked-ballot system. That's a process where voters list candidates in order of preference. If their first choice doesn't get enough votes for a majority, their second choice can be counted to help give their second choice a majority. It's not hard to see why the Liberals like this arrangement: They are probably the most likely second-choice out of all non-Liberal voters; an NDP voter will pick Liberals over Conservatives, and a lot of Conservative voters would pick Liberal as their second choice over NDP. Trudeau's voting reform sounded like a step forward for democracy. In reality it was a deeply cynical ploy to ensure that the votes that counted the most were for Liberals, and that the self-proclaimed natural governing party would firmly entrench its control over Ottawa.

The trouble was, Trudeau's voting-reform committee strangely refused to play along with his scheme. After all the town halls and surveys, the committee recommended a proportional representation system, and suggested it be put against the current system in a national referendum.[15]

But the Liberals didn't want a referendum. And they definitely didn't want proportional representation to replace first-past-the-post. Quite the opposite; it would be a nightmare for them. Proportional representation is the enemy of "big tent" brokerage parties like the Liberals who have a history of trying to be all things to all people.

---

15   Aaron Wherry and John Paul Tasker, "Minister 'disappointed' as electoral reform committee recommends referendum on proportional representation," CBC News, Dec. 1, 2016, *https://www.cbc.ca/news/politics/wherry-electoral-reform-committee-1.3866879.*

That's because proportional representation tries to make sure every vote counts completely not by ranking, but by allotting seats based on the number of votes — not just who got the most votes. The result in countries that use proportional representation is that smaller parties tend to get into parliament more easily simply by mobilizing enough enthusiasm among a small group of supporters over a single issue. It actually weakens the power of parties like the Liberals by drawing off voters who would rather elect someone from a smaller party with a clear stand than someone from a larger party that stands for, well, not much.

Trudeau had pretended he was open to all the options. He was lying. The Liberal platform even said proportional representation was an option, when it promised that, "We will convene an all-party Parliamentary committee to review a wide variety of reforms, such as ranked ballots, proportional representation, mandatory voting, and online voting."[16] It wasn't an option. They were lying. Trudeau insisted to Maclean's as the process was beginning that his preference didn't matter, and that it would be up to the people to decide on the system they wanted. "And it's not up to any one person, even if it's the prime minister, to define exactly what that right system is," Trudeau said.[17]

He was lying.

Maryam Monsef was the Liberal minister in charge of democratic reform at the time. You know Maryam Monsef: She's the same Liberal who was proudly touted by Trudeau as the first Afghan-Canadian MP, but it later turned out she was actually from Iran and may have immigrated here with a false refugee claim.[18] That only came to light, by the way, when *The Globe and Mail* exposed it, not because she

---

16   Liberal Party, 2015 Platform, "Electoral Reform," *https://www.liberal.ca/ realchange/electoral-reform/*.

17   Paul Wells, "Justin Trudeau on electoral reform: Maybe consistency isn't the word," *Maclean's*, Feb. 1, 2018, *https://www.macleans.ca/politics/ottawa/justin-trudeau-on-electoral-reform-maybe-consistency-isnt-the-word/*.

18   Candice Malcolm, "The Maryam Monsef double standard," *Toronto Sun*, Oct. 3, 2016, *https://torontosun.com/2016/10/03/the-maryam-monsef-double-standard/ wcm/acfca3ed-3772-4383-b781-67aa9a654880*.

volunteered it. And Monsef claimed she was unaware of all this, which sure makes you wonder how reporters figured out where she was born before she apparently did. Anyway, the woman elected claiming a false biography who came to Canada on false claim, that's the person Trudeau put in charge of overseeing the overhaul of Canada's entire system of democracy.

Or, as it turned out, failing to overhaul it. On October 19, 2016, one year to the day after Trudeau's Liberals were elected, the prime minister told *Le Devoir* that now that the Harper Conservatives were gone, there wasn't as much appetite for electoral reform.[19] That's because electoral reform was really all about making it easier for Liberal governments to get elected. And now they already were. "Under Stephen Harper, there were so many people unhappy with the government and their approach that people were saying, 'It will take electoral reform to no longer have a government we don't like,'" he said. "But under the current system, they now have a government they're more satisfied with and the motivation to change the electoral system is less compelling."[20]

By February 2017, the Liberals announced they would no longer pursue their plan for democratic reform.[21] Contrary to their platform promise — one that had been reiterated no less than 1,813 times over the election campaign and was a big part of getting the Liberals elected — 2015 would not be "the last federal election conducted under the first-past-the-post voting system."[22] Monsef blamed the committee for not giving her the answer she wanted. "They did not complete the hard work we had expected them to," Monsef told the House in 2016. "On

19   Marie Vastel, "Trudeau ne garantit plus une réforme électorale majeure," *Le Devoir*, Oct. 19, 2016, *https://www.ledevoir.com/politique/canada/482514/la-reforme-electorale-n-est-plus-garantie*.

20   BJ Siekierski, "Trudeau taking heat for walking back electoral reform," iPolitics, Oct. 19, 2016, *https://ipolitics.ca/2016/10/19/trudeau-backing-away-from-voting-system-change/*.

21   Stone, "Trudeau."

22   John Ivison, "Scuttled electoral reform betrays those who saw Trudeau as antidote to political cynicism," *National Post*, Feb. 1, 2017, *https://nationalpost.com/opinion/john-ivison-scuttled-electoral-reform-betrays-those-who-saw-trudeau-as-antidote-to-political-cynicism*.

the hard choices that we asked the committee to make, Mr. Speaker, they took a pass."[23]

Of course, the committee had done no such thing. What it had done was independently recommended proportional representation, which happened to be what the NDP favoured, and putting any change to a national referendum, which happened to be what the Conservative Party was demanding. What it didn't do was deliver to Trudeau on a silver platter the Liberal-friendly scheme he wanted all along. And so the former champion of electoral reform suddenly turned into the loudest critic of proportional representation. The democratic reform that his party once suggested could be an option in its platform was suddenly rebranded as a threat to democracy. "I came to very clearly believe that a form of proportional representation would be harmful to Canada," Trudeau now says. "I will not move towards any form of proportional representation, but if people want to talk about a different system that might benefit Canadians, like a preferential ballot, I'd be open to that."[24]

How very open and accountable. If you're a citizen who wants to talk about bringing in the voting system the Liberals prefer, because it improves their election odds, then they're completely open to hearing from Canadians all about it. Want to talk about a different kind of electoral reform, one that doesn't ensure the fix is in for the Liberal Party? Get lost, citizen.

His utter betrayal of his own voters and his own party's platform is just the most obnoxious example of Trudeau's lies about how he would clean up government, but the list of broken promises on accountability and reform goes on and on.

He promised to end the use of omnibus bills, which are packed with hundreds of pages with new legislation, much of it unrelated to the stated purpose of the bill — easier to sneak in laws that the opposition

---

23   Wherry and Tasker, "Minister."

24   Elise von Scheel, "A year later, Trudeau will only revisit electoral reform if pushed by other parties — something MPs don't buy," CBC News, Feb. 1, 2018, *https://www.cbc.ca/news/politics/trudeau-electoral-reform-january-2018-1.4511902.*

parties and journalists won't notice if they're buried at the bottom of page 287. Hey, and even if they happen to find it, there are too many pages and too many things in the bill for Parliament to properly digest and debate them before the government moves it to passage. "Stephen Harper has also used omnibus bills to prevent Parliament from properly reviewing and debating his proposals. We will change the House of Commons Standing Orders to bring an end to this undemocratic practice," the Liberals accused in their 2015 election platform. "We will ... bring an end to this undemocratic practice."[25]

They were lying.

In fact, the Liberals have made even better use of the omnibus trick to get past those pesky Parliamentarians than the Harper government ever did. Their 2019 budget was 319 pages long. Buried in those pages were important changes to law that were completely unrelated to the budget: There were changes to refugee claim rules for asylum seekers; there were changes to the land zoning for ski hills in Banff National Park; there was an increase in court appointment numbers.[26] All of Budget 2016 was 413 pages.[27] All of Budget 2017 was 607 pages.

And the 2018 budget clocked in at 582 pages, which included deep within them a special new law that was a favour to the Liberals' friends at SNC-Lavalin. That Quebec-based engineering company, charged with corruption and bribery offences, had needed a change to Canadian law that would allow them to avoid trial and charges if they undertook certain measures to clean up their corporate rot. Good luck finding that on page 527. It was so well hidden that even government MPs didn't know it was there. Liberal MP Greg Fergus told the House of

---

25   Liberal Party, 2015 Platform, "Prorogation and Omnibus Bills," *https://www.liberal.ca/realchange/prorogation-and-omnibus-bills/*.

26   "Justin Trudeau needs to stop borrowing Stephen Harper's omnibus trick," *Maclean's*, May 13, 2019, *https://www.macleans.ca/opinion/justin-trudeau-needs-to-stop-borrowing-stephen-harpers-omnibus-trick/*.

27   Rachel Alello, "Morneau's office doesn't consider 556-page budget bill omnibus," CTV News, March 28, 2018, *https://www.ctvnews.ca/politics/morneau-s-office-doesn-t-consider-556-page-budget-bill-omnibus-1.3862652*.

Commons finance committee that he had serious concerns about the change but had missed it completely in his review of the budget.

"I do have some serious questions about this," Fergus said. "It seems we're letting those with the means have an easier time of it than those who don't have the means." And although "he had read through most of the large budget bill before the committee hearing, he hadn't seen the deferred prosecution provision," the CBC reported.[28] No kidding, Greg. Slipping special favours for Liberal cronies past unsuspecting Parliamentarians was the plan all along.

But not to worry. Finance Minister Bill Morneau has a great excuse for why he's still using these gargantuan omnibus bills to slide past Parliament any number of Trudeau's pet policies. It's simple, he said: These aren't actually omnibus bills. "Our bills are big because they are getting a lot done for middle-class Canadians," his spokesperson told CTV News.[29] Of course. Obviously making special plea deals available for Liberal corporate cronies ranks high on the list of concerns of middle-class Canadians.

By stacking these changes inside budget bills, Greg Fergus and the entire Liberal caucus had no choice but to vote in favour of every last page of it as a "traditional confidence matter," one of the only exceptions Trudeau said he would make to allowing free votes by his MPs.[30] (Money bills are considered confidence measures.) But then, it turns out Trudeau never followed through on the promise of allowing free votes for most bills, either. The Liberals' election platform had said that the party's individual MPs would be required to vote along with the government only on bills that "implement the Liberal electoral platform," that were "traditional confidence matters, like the budget," and "those that address … protections guaranteed by the Charter of Rights and Freedoms." But when New Brunswick Liberal MP Wayne

---

28   Andy Blatchford, "Federal budget bill quietly proposes tool to ease penalties for corporate crime," CBC News, May 15, 2018, *https://www.cbc.ca/news/politics/ federal-budget-corporate-wrongdoing-1.4664490*.

29   Alello, "Morneau's."

30   Liberal Party, 2015 Platform, "Free Votes," *https://www.liberal.ca/ realchange/free-votes/*.

Long tried testing that commitment and voted against Trudeau's wishes on changes to small-business taxes (which was clearly not a confidence bill), Trudeau punished him for breaking ranks.[31] All Long had done was vote with the Conservatives to extend the consultation period on the changes. Long had said he needed to vote for his constituents, and since his riding had the heaviest concentration of small businesses and also many doctors with medical corporations, he had to oppose the changes. For that, Trudeau kicked him off the committees Long was sitting on: the standing committee on human resources, skills, social development and the status of persons with disabilities, as well as the standing committee on access to information, privacy and ethics. All because he had done, in the words of Trudeau's eviscerated promise, what MPs were "elected to do — represent their communities in Parliament and hold the government to account."

Now, of all the outrages committed by Trudeau's government, its blatant and cynical hypocrisy over its democratic reform promises probably doesn't rank anywhere near the top for most of us. After all, changing the electoral system that risked trading our century-old tried-and-true democratic institution for the same mess of a system we see in countries like Italy was a dangerous gimmick, no matter where it ended up. But Trudeau's complete betrayal of those who naively expected he would actually be accountable and transparent is important to highlight because it's the background for his entire modus operandi. Resurrecting the entitlement culture of the old Librano era simply wouldn't be possible if the prime minister actually kept his promises to be truly accountable and transparent. Not if he allowed citizens and journalists to file more Access to Information requests. Not if he couldn't sneak favours for his friends into omnibus bills. Not if he allowed MPs to vote on behalf of their constituents, rather than toeing the Trudeau line.

If Wayne Long still managed to defy his own government even after he was warned ahead of time he would be punished, imagine how

---

31   Bobbi-Jean MacKinnon, "New Brunswick MP kicked off 2 committees for breaking Liberal ranks on tax changes," CBC News, Oct. 5, 2017, *https:// www.cbc.ca/news/canada/new-brunswick/wayne-long-liberal-mp-committee-business-tax-1.4342744.*

many disobedient MPs might feel liberated to interfere with the prime minister's agenda if they didn't risk their careers in doing so? Imagine how many would have broken ranks, for example, over the SNC-Lavalin scandal.

Of course, we don't have to imagine what would have happened to Liberal MPs who chose to value their public service and their constituents over their party loyalty. We saw what happened to two female cabinet ministers when they had the temerity to talk back to Trudeau about SNC-Lavalin. Former Attorney General Jody Wilson-Raybould was demoted and then evicted from caucus, along with former Indian Affairs minister Jane Philpott, who had resigned from cabinet in solidarity with Wilson-Raybould. Trudeau then banned them from running for the Liberals in the 2019 election.

Two senior cabinet ministers, it turns out, were just two more suckers who fell for Trudeau's promises of better governance.

You only have to read the statements the two women released after being fired to see how much they believed him, and how little they should have. "I ran to be a Member of Parliament for the purpose of improving people's lives," Philpott wrote after she had been ejected.[32] "I thought there should be scope within the caucus and the party for a range of views on the SNC-Lavalin case including the views I expressed directly to the Prime Minister." How wrong she was.

"When I got involved" in the Liberal Party, Wilson-Raybould said after the ouster,[33] "I believed that we would be doing politics differently. That each member of Parliament would have a role to play in public policy and lawmaking. That members of cabinet would be able to determine the way forward and lead the files." But that's not how it happened.

---

32   "Jane Philpott posts Facebook statement after ouster from Liberal caucus," *Georgia Straight*, April 2, 2019, *https://www.straight.com/news/1222801/jane-philpott-posts-facebook-statement-after-ouster-liberal-caucus*.

33   "JWR on Liberal Party: I thought we would be doing politics differently," Global News video, May 27, 2019, *https://www.msn.com/en-ca/news/other/jwr-on-liberal-party-i-thought-we-would-be-doing-politics-differently/vi-AABZjAn*.

The opinions of members of Parliament and their constituents aren't what matters in the new Librano regime any more than they mattered in the last one. The Trudeau Liberal government isn't about representing Canadians; it's about the perks, power and money, including the illegal kind. Especially the illegal kind. And the boss himself and his family didn't waste any time in breaking the law so they could start the process of enriching themselves the very first year of his mandate, by essentially arranging to receive what, under Canadian law, is effectively considered an illegal bribe.

It happened just a short while after he became prime minister. The Trudeaus contacted the family of the Aga Khan, the billionaire Ismaili spiritual leader, to ask for a gift. They wanted to have a family vacation on the Aga Khan's private island in the Bahamas for spring break in March 2016. They made the demand within the first few months of Trudeau being sworn in.[34]

Of course they did: The 349-acre private island, called Bell Island, is located in the gorgeous Exuma Cays Land and Sea Park of the Bahamas, a playground for pampered celebrities like Johnny Depp and Richard Branson, both of whom own islands there, among dozens of other A-list jet-setters that Trudeau would no doubt consider his kind of people.[35] The CBC obtained pictures and video of the Bell Island tropical retreat and described it as "an idyllic location.[36] An elegant, modern cream-coloured main house. A landscaped terrace surrounded by tropical flowers overlooking the water. Waterfront gazebos with thatched roofs and wooden pathways leading to ocean lookouts." The

---

34   Licia Corbella, "Trudeau may be first sitting PM slammed in ethics breach, but he's not the worst," *Calgary Herald*, Dec. 27, 2017, *https://calgaryherald.com/ news/politics/corbella-trudeau-may-be-first-sitting-pm-slammed-in-ethics-breach-but-hes-not-the-worst.*

35   "Exuma: The Secret Celebrity Hideaway," *Exuma Online*, June 1, 2017, *http://exuma.online/entertainment/exuma-secret-celebrity-hideaway/.*

36   Elizabeth Thompson, "Aga Khan island that hosted Trudeau owned by company with offshore ties, records show," CBC News, May 16, 2017, *https://www. cbc.ca/news/politics/bell-island-bahamas-ownership-aga-khan-1.4115531.*

island is also home to the Aga Khan's $250 million, 150-foot super yacht.[37] Who wouldn't want a vacation there? Especially a free one?

The trouble is, the Aga Khan isn't just another celebrity billionaire with a private island. He also does business with the Canadian government through his foundation. It's actually a registered lobbyist; the foundation actively lobbied the federal government over its desire to build a "Centre for Pluralism" located alongside the Ottawa River, and for federal funds to revitalize the riverside area around it.[38] In fact, in November 2015, the Aga Khan connected with Trudeau at a climate conference, just after Trudeau had become prime minister, and discussed the project with him.[39] And since 2004, federal taxpayers have written $310 million in cheques to support the Aga Khan Foundation's foreign aid projects. Trudeau's government gave it $55 million for aid work in Afghanistan.

So Trudeau knew full well that the Aga Khan had business with the Canadian government. That it had lobbied for public money for its projects. So this was no innocent oversight. Trudeau's family had explicitly sought a personal favour from a lobbyist. A very valuable personal favour. Since no one can really even buy a vacation at the billionaire's private island, you might even call it a priceless gift.

But Trudeau wasn't about to tell anyone about it. It was supposed to be a secret gift. Considered in that context, this was a more self-serving form of graft than even the original Libranos had pulled off. The Chrétien government had funnelled booty to the party and to Liberal friends; Trudeau was now taking it for himself. And make no mistake, under Canadian law, this was absolutely illegal.

---

37   David Akin, "Trudeau and family were New Year's guests of the Aga Khan on his private Bahamas island," *National Post*, Jan. 6, 2017, *https://nationalpost.com/news/politics/trudeau-and-family-were-new-years-guests-of-the-aga-khan-on-his-private-bahamas-island.*

38   John Ivison, "Trudeau may feel like Achilles, but his heel of entitlement was pierced after conflict of interest ruling," *National Post*, Dec. 20, 2017, *https://nationalpost.com/opinion/john-ivison-trudeau-may-feel-like-achilles-but-his-heel-of-entitlement-was-pierced-after-conflict-of-interest-ruling.*

39   ibid.

But it didn't stop after spring break. His wife, former Quebec TV celebrity, amateur singer and yoga enthusiast Sophie Gregoire, got in touch with the Aga Khan's daughter to arrange another trip over the Christmas break.[40] Again: they weren't being invited. They weren't being offered the gift. They were just brazenly asking for it. And so they went again, flown in as usual on the billionaire's private helicopter. They even "exchanged gifts" there, according to details of the trip that would emerge later.[41]

And Trudeau tried to keep it all hush-hush. No wonder. Not only is it illegal under Canadian law, the whole thing reeks of corruption. Is there anything more obviously corrupt than a sitting prime minister accepting multiple gifts, including priceless vacations, from a lobbyist who has business in seeking funding from the federal government?

The *Toronto Sun*'s David Akin reported on New Year's Day 2017 that the prime minister was strangely out of the country while his ministers had been left behind to ring in the momentous New Year that was Canada's 150th.[42] Trudeau's press people would not say where he was. This despite Trudeau posting a New Year's message that January 1, 2016 was, "150 years in the making and a once-in-a-lifetime opportunity to ring in the New Year together." He had also prerecorded a video greeting about it. But the prime minister himself wasn't actually here to be together with Canadians. He was somewhere else, and he wasn't saying where. Akin wrote: "This year, Trudeau's office is keeping his destination closely guarded and would not, when asked Saturday, say what country he will be in to usher in the year in which Canada will mark the 150th anniversary of Confederation. Nor would his aides say what continent or even hemisphere he will be in when he wakes up on the first day of 2017."

---

40   ibid.

41   ibid.

42   David Akin, "Trudeau holidays in another country as Canada begins celebrating 'once-in-a-lifetime' anniversary," *Toronto Sun*, Jan. 1, 2017, *https:// torontosun.com/2017/01/01/trudeau-holidays-in-another-country-as-canada-begins-celebrating-once-in-a-lifetime-anniversary/wcm/b56960d2-b742-413b-939e-c96cf16919c4.*

Under pressure, the Prime Minister's Office eventually gave a slightly less vague answer and admitted he was in Nassau. That's the Bahamian capital. It's also a popular tourist destination — for normal tourists. With hotels and resorts for normal tourists. Maybe even normal politicians. That little tidbit of information seemed to be enough for some people. The *National Post*'s Chris Selley wrote on January 4 about how, after learning the Nassau nugget, reporters were now being pressured to drop the matter. "Knowing the location would be a security risk, some tweeted. We in the media would just find something else to complain about. The Trudeaus deserve privacy just like everyone else. (For heaven's sake, we weren't asking for their room numbers.)" Selley wrote.[43] "The difficulty of accessing basic information about the Canadian government is a long-running scandal; Trudeau promised to do better on this front, and 'where the Prime Minister is' is about as basic and routine as information gets. That's why the media care, and that's why you should care too." Then, after writing the column, Selley got a secret tip. Someone leaked to him the truth that the Trudeaus were on the private island of the Aga Khan.

Not Nassau. That was a lie. It's about 100 kilometres from Nassau, actually. Across a lot of ocean.

The Prime Minister's Office refused to confirm it at first.[44] Then they finally confessed, only to try lying their way out of it. "As you are aware, his Highness (the Aga Khan) and the Prime Minister have been close family friends for many years," came the official statement from the PMO. And when Trudeau was caught, he stuck with that line. They were good friends. It was just friends having a vacation together, one a billionaire playboy born into quasi-royalty, the other a public servant of the Canadian people. "I've always considered the Aga Khan a close family friend," Trudeau said, "which is why I didn't clear this family trip in the first place," with the commissioner for conflict of

43   Chris Selley, "It's 2017. Do you know where your prime minister is?, *National Post*, Jan. 3, 2017," National Post, *https://nationalpost.com/opinion/chris-selley-its-2017-do-you-know-where-your-prime-minister-is*.

44   Chris Selley, "Justin Trudeau's vacation with the Aga Khan proves the details matter," *National Post*, Jan. 6, 2017, *https://nationalpost.com/opinion/chris-selley-justin-trudeaus-vacation-with-the-aga-khan-proves-the-details-matter*.

interest and ethics.[45] Even if that claim were true, clearing it anyway might have been the kind of behaviour Canadians might have expected from a prime minister promising transparency and accountability. But he didn't just choose not to clear it with the commissioner; he tried to hide the trip from everybody.

The claim that he and the Aga Khan were old chums was merely Trudeau's desperate attempt to get around the law. The Conflict of Interest Act is explicit that, "No public office holder or member of his or her family shall accept any gift or other advantage, including from a trust, that might reasonably be seen to have been given to influence the public office holder in the exercise of an official power, duty or function."[46] Doing so is therefore, by definition illegal, never mind blatantly unethical. This law was brought in by the Harper government after the Chrétien years specifically with an eye on catching nefarious Librano-like behaviour. The law only makes a few exceptions, including if the gift or favour is "given by a relative or friend." Trudeau claimed he and the Aga Khan were old pals since his dad and the billionaire had also been friends. His dad had taken him on vacation in Greece with the Aga Khan's family when Trudeau was 12 and, "I have seen him many times since then for dinners at his place," Trudeau said.[47]

Trudeau was lying again.

Ethics commissioner Mary Dawson investigated the trip once it came to light and in December 2017, a year after the Trudeaus had been secretly island hopping on the Aga Khan's helicopter to his tropical Shangri-

---

45   Lucas Holtvluwer, "RCMP asked to investigate Trudeau's trips to Aga Khan's island," *The Post Millennial*, May 2019, *https://www.thepostmillennial.com/rcmp-asked-to-investigate-trudeaus-trips-to-aga-khans-island/*.

46   Conflict of Interest Act, Part 1, *https://laws-lois.justice.gc.ca/eng/acts/C-36.65/page-2.html#h-92089*.

47   Peter Zimonjic and Kathleen Harris, "2014 visit to Aga Khan's island was also by private helicopter, Trudeau says," CBC News, Jan. 24, 2017, *https://www.cbc.ca/news/politics/aga-khan-2014-trip-1.3950714*.

La, she issued a report that shredded Trudeau's story to pieces.[48] Far from being friends, Trudeau had no interactions with the Aga Khan since that trip from his childhood until after he became Liberal leader, with the exception of when he saw him at Pierre Trudeau's funeral.[49] "The evidence shows that, but for the Aga Khan's attendance at Mr. Trudeau's father's funeral in 2000, Mr. Trudeau had no private or personal interactions with the Aga Khan between 1983 and the fall of 2013, a span of 30 years," Dawson wrote.[50] There were no "dinners at his place." Justin Trudeau was lying through his teeth.

Dawson also discovered that the Aga Khan's family wasn't even on the island the first time the Trudeaus were there, fully exposing the lie that this was a vacation of family friends. They were told the billionaire's clan wouldn't even be there over the Christmas holiday. "The evidence also shows that during the March 2016 trip, no member of the Aga Khan's family was on the island and that, during the planning for the December 2016 trip, the Trudeaus were informed that the Aga Khan and his family may or may not be present," Dawson wrote in her report. "These circumstances do not suggest that Mr. Trudeau and the Aga Khan were seeking to fulfil opportunities to spend private time together as friends."[51]

When Dawson asked Trudeau why he had so little contact with this supposedly close friend, Trudeau claimed because when he was just a lowly teacher, he didn't consider himself to be high-status enough to have a relationship with a billionaire, quasi-prince. It was only when he became a powerful politician that he was comfortable rekindling the friendship. That must have been some genuine friendship if it was strictly based on how much power each one possessed.

---

48   Mary Dawson, *The Trudeau Report made under the Conflict of Interest Act and Conflict of Interest Code for Members of the House of Commons*, Office of the Conflict of Interest and Ethics Commissioner, Dec. 20, 2017, *http://ciec-ccie. parl.gc.ca/Documents/English/Public%20Reports/Examination%20Reports/The%20 Trudeau%20Report.pdf.*

49   John Ivison, "Trudeau."

50   Dawson, *The Trudeau.*

51   ibid.

Why else would the Aga Khan be so generous with his vacation gifts if he wasn't trying to curry favour with the current prime minister, whom his foundation was actively lobbying? "I also see it as unlikely that the invitation would have been given to Mr. Trudeau or his family had there not been official interaction between the government of Canada and the Aga Khan and had Mr. Trudeau not become a significant player on the Canadian political scene," Dawson wrote. [52]

In fact, Dawson realized, that power-hungry fake friendship that Trudeau described was exactly the kind of greasy relationship the conflict-of-interest law was meant for. "In my view, Mr. Trudeau's description of his own friendship with the Aga Khan suggests that it arose as a result of his position as the Leader of the Liberal Party of Canada and subsequently from his position as Prime Minister," she wrote. She added: "Private interactions between Mr. Trudeau and the Aga Khan developed only after Mr. Trudeau became a leading political figure in Canada and the nature of these interactions fails to suggest a relationship as friends that can appropriately be characterized as one contemplated by subsection 11(2) of the Act." [53]

That wasn't the only illegal act Dawson discovered. She found Trudeau in violation of four provisions of the Conflict of Interest Act. These are the provisions stated in the act:[54]

"Every public office holder shall arrange his or her private affairs in a manner that will prevent the public office holder from being in a conflict of interest." Trudeau did not.

"No public office holder or member of his or her family shall accept any gift or other advantage, including from a trust, that might reasonably be seen to have been given to influence the public office holder in the exercise of an official power, duty or function." Trudeau had done just that.

---

52   ibid.

53   ibid.

54   Conflict of Interest Act, Part 1.

"No minister of the Crown, minister of state or parliamentary secretary, no member of his or her family and no ministerial adviser or ministerial staff shall accept travel on non-commercial chartered or private aircraft for any purpose unless required in his or her capacity as a public office holder or in exceptional circumstances or with the prior approval of the Commissioner." Trudeau was island hopping on the private helicopter of a billionaire.

"A public office holder shall recuse himself or herself from any discussion, decision, debate or vote on any matter in respect of which he or she would be in a conflict of interest." Trudeau had met with the Aga Khan on Parliament Hill in May 2016 — after he was already in a severe conflict of interest over the spring break trip.[55] He was breaking the law, and he just didn't care.

---

55   Aaron Wherry, "For Justin Trudeau, a vacation on the Aga Khan's island was not worth the trip," CBC News, Dec. 20, 2017, *https://www.cbc.ca/news/politics/trudeau-aga-khan-ethics-island-analysis-wherry-1.4458606.*

CHAPTER 3

BILL MORNEAU, THE LIBRANO BANKER

Justin Trudeau was the first sitting prime minister in Canadian who was personally caught breaking federal law.[56] And not just in one infraction: He broke it in four different ways.

That's not what he thinks, of course. Trudeau and his new Libranos don't think laws actually apply to them. His jet setting finance minister, Bill Morneau — who actually married into a family of Canadian billionaires with his wife Nancy McCain (of the frozen French fry fortune), and is a multi-millionaire himself thanks to the company his fath   er started — flouted government ethics rules for years.

Morneau owns a villa in the south of France, another one of those sunny billionaire playgrounds (the Aga Khan's family once had a villa

---

56   Jim Bronskill, "Baloney meter: Is Justin Trudeau's ethics breach a first in Canadian history?" CTV News, Jan. 25, 2018, *https://www.ctvnews.ca/politics/baloney-meter-is-justin-trudeau-s-ethics-breach-a-first-in-canadian-history-1.3775004.*

there, too, but later sold it to the Saudi royal family[57]). It was owned through a private corporation, which Morneau has a few of, often used as a way of minimizing his own tax bill; (the finance minister prefers to maximize everyone's tax bill but his own). [58]

MPs are supposed to disclose any private companies they own to the ethics and conflict of interest commissioner. The reason is obvious. If a politician has a private business interest, there is always the possibility that he could be making decisions while in government to benefit that business. But Morneau didn't disclose the company that owned the villa to the commissioner for two years. He just didn't. He had owned the company since 2007, but he chose not to tell the ethics commissioner anything about it at all. He just chose to keep it a secret. It wasn't until the CBC discovered it and began asking him about it, that he finally filed notice of its existence with the office of ethics and conflict of interest commissioner.[59] He was hiding it. For two years.

The thing is, when you are in a position of power and trust, and when you make policy decisions about taxes, and investments, and money, you have to tell the ethics commissioner about your own holdings.[60] Not all of it will be published: Some of it can be kept private between you and the ethics commissioner. But you have to disclose it, so an independent officer knows if you're passing laws that would benefit yourself or your family. If you don't like it, if you don't want to tell your personal wealth secrets, that's no problem — then don't become finance minister. It's invasive, I'm sure; a millionaire who married a billionaire and has a fancy villa in France would surely like his privacy.

---

57   "Château de l'Horizon," Wikipedia, *https://en.wikipedia.org/wiki/ Ch%C3%A2teau_de_l%27Horizon.*

58   Philip Cross, "Trudeau and Morneau understand tax dodging. They do it, too," *Financial Post*, Nov. 30, 2017, *https://business.financialpost.com/opinion/philip-cross-trudeau-and-morneau-understand-tax-dodging-they-do-it-too.*

59   Elizabeth Thompson, "Finance Minister Bill Morneau waited 2 years to disclose company that owns his French villa to ethics watchdog," CBC News, Oct. 13, 2017, *https://www.cbc.ca/news/politics/morneau-company-france-ethics-1.4351933.*

60   Office of the Conflict of Interest and Ethics Commissioner, "Welcome to the Office," *http://ciec-ccie.parl.gc.ca/EN/Pages/default.aspx.*

Fine — then don't take the job of setting rules that affect millionaires who marry billionaires who have fancy villas in France.

He had to disclose it. He swore that he disclosed things. But he lied. He lied for two years, until he was caught.[61] He only confessed when reporters started asking about it. Now, how do you think the Canada Revenue Agency would react to you if you just "forgot" to tell them about a valuable asset for two years? I'm not saying Morneau is hiding this from the tax man — I'm saying he hid it from the ethics commissioner. Just like Trudeau hid his illegal gift of a private island vacation from the ethics commissioner.

Of course, Morneau has been dogged by allegations of secrecy, misleading the public and severe conflicts of interest even with businesses that everyone knew he owned. When he became finance minister, it was expected he'd put his substantial stake in his father's company Morneau Shepell in a blind trust or sell them. So everyone assumed he had. Politicians in a position of power are supposed to place their assets in a blind trust, managed by someone else completely at arm's length, with no communication about what is being done with the investment, or they sell them completely in an equally arm's length transaction. Ministers have to pick one or the other within 120 days of being appointed.[62]

And yet Morneau simply didn't pick either. He chose to ignore the rule. He kept his shares and stayed an active shareholder for nearly two years after he was appointed finance minister. He hid behind the reason that because his Morneau Shepell shares, like his villa, were owned through a holding company (used for tax purposes — not like a

---

61   Thompson, "Finance."

62   Robert Fife and Steven Chase, "Bill Morneau didn't place assets in blind trust, raising conflict-of-interest risk," *The Globe and Mail*, Oct. 16, 2017, *https:// www.theglobeandmail.com/news/politics/finance-minister-bill-morneau-didnt-place-assets-in-blind-trust-raising-conflict-of-interest-risk/article36596635/*.

blind trust), they weren't directly "controlled" by him — even though it was his very own holding company.[63]

Again, the reasons for having these rules here are so painfully obvious. A politician in a position of power can do all kinds of things to benefit a company he happens to own a big chunk of. Putting those holdings in a blind trust doesn't completely solve the problem, of course. It only makes sure that the politician isn't actively involved in the business and privy to internal company communication and information. That only reduces the potential for conflict, it doesn't eliminate it. It's the minimum step a politician in power can take to diminish the perception of conflict. Remember that clause in the Conflict of Interest Act that Trudeau was found to have violated: "Every public office holder shall arrange his or her private affairs in a manner that will prevent the public office holder from being in a conflict of interest." That's *every* public office holder. But Morneau isn't just any public office holder. He's the finance minister. He's the second-most powerful cabinet minister in the country after the prime minister himself. The finance minister is in charge of the very policies that most affect the business and investment decisions of companies, with the power to adjust tax rates, credits and subsidies.

It's important to note that this is no small holding we're talking about. Bill Morneau had inherited a substantial chunk of the firm from his father and the company had grown to be a very successful one. Morneau's personal shares were worth as much as $40 million, maybe more.[64] That gave him a very big interest in the future success of Morneau Shepell. All the more reason you would think he would at least put it in a blind trust, given his ability as finance minister to use policy to impact that future success. But he didn't. He kept the shares. He remained an active shareholder. And he just kept quiet about it.

---

63   John Geddes, "Here's why Bill Morneau didn't sell his stock or set up a blind trust," *Maclean's*, Oct. 17, 2017, *https://www.macleans.ca/politics/ottawa/heres-why-bill-moreau-didnt-sell-his-stock-or-set-up-a-blind-trust/*.

64   Fife and Chase, "Bill."

He didn't breathe a word about it to the public — right up until the moment he was caught.[65]

That atrociously unethical decision — and the choice to mislead the public about it — was bad enough. But Morneau Shepell is not just any other run-of-the-mill company, either. It wasn't just influenced by the same tax and fiscal policies as every other corporation. For one thing, Morneau Shepell is just one of a handful of major firms in the Canadian human-resources and pension-management sector. Its business is administering pensions for companies that are its clients. As finance minister, Morneau personally oversees pension rules that would affect the way that Morneau Shepell manages those pensions. And, in October 2016, Morneau actually introduced a dramatic new change to pension rules. Bill C-27 would make it possible for federally regulated employers (for instance, Canada Post) to replace their lavish defined-benefit pensions with less generous targeted-benefit pension plans, where there's less of a guarantee of a rich retirement.[66]

What a funny coincidence. Before Morneau got into politics, he was the executive chairman of Morneau Shepell, where he publicly advocated for replacing defined-benefit plans, which have in many cases become financially unsustainable, with targeted-benefit plans.[67] Those plans, which are called a "hybrid" between defined-benefit (DB) and defined-contribution (DC) plans, are just the kind of plans that a company like Morneau Shepell is considered one of the key firms in administering.[68] Why, it's right there in the company sales pitch on its website: "We are the recognized leader in handling multi-employer plans, plans

---

65   ibid.

66   Julie Cazzen, "Bill C-27 could mean changes for DB pensions," MoneySense, Jan. 6, 2017, https://www.moneysense.ca/save/retirement/pensions/defined-benefit-pension-plans-due-change/.

67   Steven Chase and Robert Fife, "Morneau didn't seek clearance from ethics commissioner before introducing pension bill," *The Globe and Mail, https://www.theglobeandmail.com/news/politics/morneau-didnt-seek-clearance-from-ethics-commissioner-before-introducing-pension-bill/article37036038/.*

68   Lindsay McGlashan, "The Target Benefit Plan: An Emerging Pension Regime," Library of Parliament Research Paper, 2016-20E March 11, 2016, *https://lop.parl.ca/sites/PublicWebsite/default/en_CA/ResearchPublications/201620E.*

where sponsors want control of their investment options, and complex integrated retirement plans with DC, defined benefit (DB), or hybrid components."[69] Morneau didn't even bother to clear ahead of time with the ethics commissioner whether he should be introducing a bill that so directly affected a company he partly owned.[70] Of course he didn't.

But targeted pensions are just one of many of the services Morneau Shepell offers. Another is private pension plans, for professionals, like doctors or lawyers, who don't have a company pension plan but want something like it for their retirement portfolio. That's just the kind of business that could be impacted by changes to, say, how self-employed professionals are taxed on their investments. When Morneau unleashed his tax-grab attack on small businesses in late 2017, he specifically went after the way people are taxed on their investments in their own private corporations, like the ones a lot of self-employed professionals use as vehicles to run their professions and build their retirement (your family doctor probably owns one). Tax experts quickly pointed out that raising taxes on those could prompt more professionals to turn for retirement security instead to a private pension plan. You know, like the kind sold by the very company that the finance minister partly owned.

So Morneau's potential for conflict in creating rules that would help a firm he held a stake in worth tens of millions of dollars is so screamingly obvious, there can be no way Morneau failed to appreciate it. But that's not the only way he was in a massive, ugly conflict. Morneau Shepell actually does business directly with the federal government. Between 2010 and 2017, the company, which was being led by Morneau himself for many of those years, received $53 million in federal contracts. In October 2107, at the time when Morneau was caught not publicly disclosing his continued ownership of Morneau Shepell shares, there were at least $14 million in active federal government contracts held

---

69   Morneau Shepell website, "Defined Contribution Pension Administration," accessed Aug. 17, 2019, *https://www.morneaushepell.com/ca-en/defined-contribution-pension-administration.*

70   Chase and Fife, "Morneau."

by the finance minister's then-company. One was with the Bank of Canada, which the Finance Minister directly oversees. And there were no fewer than eight contracts between Morneau Shepell and the Canada Revenue Agency. Some were signed as recently as June 2017 — just a few months before Morneau was discovered as still being an active shareholder in the company.

No one is saying the company Morneau Shepell itself did anything wrong here. If anything, the firm has plainly been unhappy with being dragged into Morneau's personal financial scandals, and even issued a statement distancing itself from its former chairman and making it clear that it has done nothing here illegal or illegitimate.[71]

The problem isn't Morneau Shepell. The problem is Bill Morneau. Any normal politician would have immediately recognized the problems in holding onto his stake while a company he partially owned was signing deals with the government and while he was passing laws that could affect the company's business.

But Morneau didn't care. He and Trudeau don't operate like normal politicians. The normal-politician rules don't apply to them. Not the rules about blind trusts. Not the rules about personal business conflicts. Not the rules about disclosing French villas. Not the rules about accepting helicopter rides from billionaires. Not the rules about accepting gifts of opulent vacations on private islands. None of them.

71   Morneau Shepell, "Statement from Morneau Shepell to clarify misinformation," press release, Canada News Wire, Oct. 27, 2017, *https:// www.newswire.ca/news-releases/statement-from-morneau-shepell-to-clarify-misinformation-653650453.html.*

CHAPTER 4

DOMINIC LEBLANC, THE GODFATHER OF NEW BRUNSWICK

Morneau and Trudeau aren't the only ones who think trifling things like federal laws and ethics rules and procedures don't apply to them. The entire Librano culture saturates the Trudeau government. Any ministers grossed out by it — like Jody Wilson-Raybould and Jane Philpott were — don't last long. But others learn to love the perks. Like Dominic LeBlanc, who like Morneau, saw no problem in a little government business going to a friendly firm. LeBlanc just happens to be an extremely close friend of Justin Trudeau's. He was originally from Ottawa, before he moved to New Brunswick, and when Trudeau was little, LeBlanc used to babysit him and his brothers.[72]

LeBlanc was caught breaking conflict of interest rules when the ethics commissioner reviewed the way LeBlanc's federal government department awarded a contract to a company backed by his wife's

---

72   "Dominic Leblanc," Wikipedia, *https://en.wikipedia.org/wiki/Dominic_LeBlanc.*

cousin. LeBlanc was fisheries minister, overseeing the granting of federal licences to commercial fishing operations. It just so happened that a very lucrative licence to harvest Arctic surf clams was available.[73] It was the fourth one that would be granted and gave the owner the right to catch up to 25 per cent of all the surf clams that were available as government-authorized catch. The surf clam is a big deal in the export market. People in Asian countries use it for sushi and other dishes.[74] And it was estimated that, for the lucky recipient, this particular licence would mean $24 million in revenue in just the first year.

The way the licence was made possible was weird to begin with: The government actually announced in September 2017 that it was taking some catch away from Nova Scotia-based Clearwater Seafoods to purportedly expand the fisheries to include Indigenous ownership.[75, 76] It was all part of its "reconciliation" effort. "The decision to introduce Indigenous participation in the Arctic Surf Clam fishery is consistent with the Government of Canada's commitment to developing a renewed relationship between Canada and Indigenous peoples," the Department of Fisheries and Oceans said in a news release.[77] "Enhancing access to the Arctic Surf Clam fishery broadens the distribution of benefits from this public resource, and is a powerful step toward reconciliation." Only, it was a completely hollow gesture: Clearwater was going to be the one paying for this reconciliation, not the government. It's like the

---

73   Kathleen Harris, "Dominic LeBlanc found in conflict of interest over lucrative fishing licence," CBC News, Sept. 12, 2018, *https://www.cbc.ca/news/ politics/leblanc-conflict-of-interest-fishing-licence-1.4820213.*

74   Clearwater website, "Arctic surf clams," accessed Aug. 17. 2019, https:// www.clearwater.ca/en/seafood-industry/clams/arctic-surf-clams/.

75   Allan Lynch, "Shake-up underway in Canada's lucrative surf clam sector," *SeafoodSource*, Oct. 9, 2017, *https://www.seafoodsource.com/news/supply-trade/shakeup- underway-in-canadas-lucrative-surf-clam-sector.*

76   Paul Withers, "Fisheries minister to Clearwater: You don't own surf clam quota," CBC News, March 7, 2018, *https://www.cbc.ca/news/canada/nova-scotia/ dominic-leblanc-surf-clam-indigenous-fisheries-1.4566712.*

77   Fisheries and Oceans Canada, "Update on Work Underway to Broaden Access to Arctic Surf Clam Fishery," press release, Canada News Wire, Aug. 10, 2018, *https://www.newswire.ca/news-releases/statement---update-on-work-underway-to- broaden-access-to-arctic-surf-clam-fishery-690577521.html.*

government choosing to reconcile with First Nations by taking your house and giving it to the nearest Indian band.

But that's what it did. It was just revoking part of Clearwater's licence. Fishing licences are really all fisheries like Clearwater have as assets, besides the processing plants. In Canada, where the government controls the fish, if you don't have a licence, you don't have a seafood business. And yet LeBlanc told the company it didn't have a "right" to all the Arctic clams. But of course that was a lie. That's what a licence is: Clearwater had secured the right to catch Arctic clams. But now LeBlanc was taking it away. The company, correctly, called it expropriation. LeBlanc acted like it wasn't because, he claimed, a licence isn't property. "You can't be expropriated from a property you don't own," he said.[78]

Then it got weirder. In December 2017, LeBlanc announced that the licence was going to something called the Five Nations Clam Corp., which claimed to have Indigenous representation from all four Atlantic provinces and Quebec. But guess what? Every one of the 13 chiefs of bands in Nova Scotia said they had no part of the Five Nations Clam Corp.[79] They all pointed out that there had been virtually no transparency about the way the licence was awarded, and demanded a review of the award, as did the provincial government of Nova Scotia.

But you know who did have a stake in the company? A relative of LeBlanc's wife, Gilles Thériault, who was her cousin. That wasn't an oversight. LeBlanc was fully aware that Thériault was involved. "In fact, Mr. Thériault raised the licensing issue with Mr. LeBlanc prior to the decision and Mr. Thériault's name appeared on the proposal submitted to Fisheries and Oceans Canada and read in full by Mr. LeBlanc," wrote ethics commissioner Mario Dion in his report on the affair.[80]

So LeBlanc knew his wife's cousin was applying for the licence. Did he recuse himself from the decision? Of course he didn't. He did the

---

78   Withers, "Fisheries."

79   ibid.

80   Harris, "Domenic."

exact opposite: He took a government licence worth tens of millions from one company, which had obtained it fair and square, and gave it to Thériault. The conflict of interest couldn't be more glaring, and yet LeBlanc, like Morneau and Trudeau, just didn't care. As Dion wrote in his report: "Public office holders are not expected to have knowledge of the private affairs of each of their birth relatives, much less those of relatives by affinity. However, when they are aware of an opportunity to further the private interests of a relative through the exercise of an official power, duty or function, they must be vigilant in taking appropriate action to avoid a conflict of interest," he wrote.[81]

LeBlanc didn't. He just flouted the rules. Flouted ethics. And, like his close friend Justin Trudeau and finance minister Bill Morneau, he hoped not to get caught. But he was. He claimed that his wife had a lot of cousins, as if that mattered.[82] The ethics commissioner found him in breach of two separate sections of the Conflict of Interest Act[83]; (the licence was subsequently cancelled and had to be given back to its original rightful owner, Clearwater [84]). LeBlanc was found to have violated subsection 6(1), which states that, "No public office holder shall make a decision or participate in making a decision related to the exercise of an official power, duty or function if the public office holder knows or reasonably should know that, in the making of the decision, he or she would be in a conflict of interest." And he violated Section 21, which requires that, "A public office holder shall recuse himself or herself from any discussion, decision, debate or vote on any matter in

---

81   ibid.

82   Steven Chase and Robert Fife, "Fisheries Minister defends decision to award clam fishing quota to company with familial, Liberal ties," *The Globe and Mail*, May 22, 2018, *https://www.theglobeandmail.com/politics/article-fisheries-minister-defends-decision-to-award-clam-fishing-quota-to/*.

83   Conflict of Interest Act, Part 1, *https://laws-lois.justice.gc.ca/eng/acts/C-36.65/page-2.html#h-92089*.

84   Holly McKenzie-Sutter, "New fisheries minister discusses reversal on controversial surf clam licence," CTV News, Aug. 14, 2018, *https://www.ctvnews.ca/politics/new-fisheries-minister-discusses-reversal-on-controversial-surf-clam-licence-1.4052802*.

respect of which he or she would be in a conflict of interest."[85] LeBlanc ignored the law. Like his fellow Libranos, he just didn't think it applied to him.

And why should he think otherwise? Leblanc has been busted time and time again engaging in the kind of sleazy ethics breaches that would make even the Clintons cringe. In 2003, when he was parliamentary secretary to the defence minister in the Chrétien government, Leblanc was discovered to have accepted private plane trips in the executive jet of New Brunswick's billionaire Irving family, and taking it to vacation at the Irving's VIP fishing lodge.[86] Amazingly, even after that scandal, Leblanc didn't stop accepting free trips on Air Irving. Just this year, it was discovered that he was using his billionaire friends' private jet to fly to medical appointments in Montreal, where he was being treated for cancer.[87] Of course, cancer is a serious disease. But that kind of first-class luxury air ambulance is not the kind of thing most Canadians get to enjoy when they're dealing with our health-care system. Anyone else would have had to make the 10-hour drive. But Leblanc doesn't choose to live like other people. He flies high — like a true Librano.

You would think his ongoing flagrant behaviour would been enough to chasten the Liberals. But that assumes they can be chastened. That they have any shame when they get caught. But they simply don't. They're shameless because they don't believe in the rules. That's why, less than a year after LeBlanc had been busted by the ethics commissioner in a patronage scandal over fishing licences, he and Trudeau were back in the news over a patronage scandal involving judicial appointments.[88]

---

85   Conflict of Interest Act, Part 1.

86   John Ivison, "Dominic LeBlanc's illness no excuse for taking advantage of his Irving connections," *National Post*, *https://nationalpost.com/opinion/john-ivison-dominic-leblancs-illness-no-excuse-for-taking-advantage-of-his-irving-connections.*

87   Brian Lilley, "LeBlanc keeps the ethics meter ticking," *Toronto Sun*, July 16, 2019, *https://torontosun.com/opinion/columnists/lilley-leblanc-keeps-the-ethics-meter-ticking.*

88   Robert Jones, "Dominic LeBlanc's family, friends, neighbour win 5 of 6 recent judicial appointments," CBC News, July 2, 2019, *https://www.cbc.ca/news/canada/new-brunswick/judicial-appointments-dominic-leblanc-family-friends-political-patronage-1.5191054.*

Ethically clean judicial appointments were another one the Trudeau Liberals' boastful promises when they took government, vowing they would appoint only the "most meritorious jurists" to the bench.[89] But in the Liberals' world, meritorious means you earn your merit based on how valuable you are to the party.

The Liberals had arranged for a smokescreen to hide the dirty way they were actually appointing judges. There are 17 seven-member advisory committees in various regions around Canada, made up of judges, lawyers, the government and some lay people, who recommend judicial picks to the government to fill vacancies on the bench.[90] The whole thing is meant to provide a sheen of integrity to appointing judges, which has the potential for being abused to reward party cronies, or to blacklist judges known for being non-friendly to the party. In reality, it is a way to cover up a whole new level of Liberal sleaze in appointing judges.

Even the original Libranos boss, Jean Chrétien, couldn't help but publicly scoff at the idea that the process was anything but rife for abuse. When it's politicians appointing judges, Chrétien told CTV in 2018, the public knows who to hold accountable for a bad pick.[91] That ministers and prime ministers can be blamed actually helps keep them more accountable, and more careful, not less so, he pointed out. Instead of making the process more transparent, Trudeau succeeded in fooling everyone by shrouding it in even greater secrecy. "Now they want committee of nobodies who will recommend, who will be responsible," Chrétien said. "You know what will happen, they said: "Name my friend I will name yours next time.' And nobody will ask a question. You cannot ask questions. You don't know who these guys (are), very often."

---

89   ibid.

90   Department of Justice Canada, "Government of Canada announces judicial appointments in the province of Ontario," press release, March 26, 2019, *https://www.canada.ca/en/department-justice/news/2019/03/government-of-canada-announces-judicial-appointments-in-the-province-of-ontario0.html*.

91   Richard Gilmore, "Chretien slams Canada's judicial appointments process," CTV News, Oct. 10, 2018, *https://www.ctvnews.ca/politics/chretien-slams-canada-s-judicial-appointments-process-1.4128845*.

And of course, the committees only recommend people: The prime minister and his inner circle still get to make the final picks from the committee's shortlist. Or not. There is nothing to say the prime minister's final picks would even have to appear on the committee's list. Given the new level of secrecy in the process, how would the public even know if a judge had appeared on a committee shortlist or not? The process could be just as dirty as before or dirtier than ever, but Trudeau's Potemkin committee process provides him with all new protections against any accusations that the whole judicial-appointment process is being used to benefit Liberals.

Which it is.

The first evidence of that came in the fallout of the SNC-Lavalin scandal, after former justice minister and attorney general Jody Wilson-Raybould had been demoted and then kicked out of caucus for refusing to be party to Trudeau's corruption of the justice system. But it had turned out that Trudeau had been showing Wilson-Raybould how ready he was to tamper in the justice system, with an entirely different disgraceful affair. It only came to light after Wilson-Raybould had been forced out, when sources leaked to the Canadian Press that Trudeau had shut down her recommendation for a top Supreme Court pick — because the judge, Glenn Joyal, wasn't an ideological Liberal.[92]

Joyal, a chief justice of Manitoba's Court of Queen's Bench, would later say that he withdrew his name from consideration for personal reasons (his wife has breast cancer).[93] But sources had told the Canadian Press that Wilson-Raybould had not only submitted a longer than 60-page memo to the prime minister arguing for Joyal's appointment to the Supreme Court seat recently vacated by former chief justice Beverley McLachlin, but that he also be appointed to the chief justice role. That

---

92   Joan Bryden, "Sources say Trudeau rejected Wilson-Raybould's conservative pick for high court," *National Observer*, March 25, 2019, *https://www. nationalobserver.com/2019/03/25/news/sources-say-trudeau-rejected-wilson-rayboulds-conservative-pick-high-court.*

93   Joan Bryden, "'This is wrong': ex-Supreme Court candidate says his candidacy is being used to further an agenda," *Global News*, March 25, 2019, *https:// globalnews.ca/news/5094485/wilson-raybould-trudeau-glenn-joyal/.*

was a big deal: The last time a judge was made chief justice without already sitting on the Supreme Court was in 1906.

There was a strong case to be made for Joyal. He was from the same region as McLachlin, which was a requirement, and he was fluently bilingual. He was widely respected as an excellent legal scholar and jurist. But there was a problem. Joyal had been appointed as Manitoba's chief justice by a Conservative: Stephen Harper. After Wilson-Raybould recommended him strongly, Trudeau had his people look into Joyal. And it turned out he was guilty of more than being just a Conservative appointee: Worse, Joyal had the temerity to think differently than the Liberal dogma. He had been publicly critical of the left-wing judicial activism that had permeated the bench in Canada. He had been critical of the Supreme Court's willingness to expand the Charter of Rights and Freedoms into areas never contemplated by the original framers or by the provinces when they had agreed to it.[94]

Joyal knew that the Charter was a compromise between then prime minister Pierre Trudeau's federal Liberal government, which badly wanted the Charter, and the premiers of the day, who were generally skeptical of the idea. He recalled correctly that the Charter had explicitly been designed to balance provincial concerns against the federal agenda by allowing the legislative branch the power to limit or override any overreaching by the judicial branch. But since then, judges had been relentlessly expanding the Charter's scope and power. As Joyal had said in a speech at the 2017 conference of the Canadian Constitution Foundation, the courts had been ignoring the intentions of the original framers.[95] Today, "the legislative branch frequently occupies a diminished and even inferior role," relative to the power of the activist judiciary, he said. This was "an unanticipated development that was not envisioned nor necessarily desired by the 1982 compromise that led to the adoption of the Charter."

---

94   Bryden, "Sources."

95   Canadian Constitutional Foundation, "Justice Glenn D. Joyal: 2017 Law and Freedom Conference keynote," March 8, 2017, *https://theccf.ca/2207-2/*.

Make no mistake: Joyal believed in the Charter. He was a champion of the Charter, which he said "deserves our respect and demands our compliance." But he understood where it came from and what it was meant to be — and, just as importantly, what its limits were meant to be. Now, he saw evolving in Canada's judicial system more than a faithfulness to the Charter: he recognized that what had happened instead was Charter activism by the courts. That, he said, has "led without question to a level of judicial potency that was not anticipated back in 1982," Joyal said. That resulted in a "less potent and less influential legislative branch that seldom has the final word." Joyal said: "With the 'constitutionalizing' of more and more political and social issues into fundamental rights, the Canadian judiciary has all but removed those issues, in a fairly permanent way, from the realm of future civic engagement and future political debate."[96]

Now that kind of thinking is rank Liberal heresy. And it is to Wilson-Raybould's credit that as a Liberal justice minister she didn't allow her party affiliation at the time to bias her own judgment in recognizing an excellent judge, even if he thought differently than she did. (Indeed, Joyal had named Wilson-Raybould in his speech specifically as someone on the Charter activism side, having called herself an "ambassador for the Charter" in her role as justice minister.)

But Trudeau is less interested in good law or diversity of thought than he is in Liberal-run courts. Sources told the Canadian Press that Wilson-Raybould's endorsement of Joyal had led to "significant disagreement" between her and Trudeau.[97] The prime minister was "disturbed" by what he learned of Joyal's independent thinking. He picked someone more in line with the Liberal brand, Sheilah Martin, an appeals judge from Alberta. Martin's career included representing the Women's Legal Education and Action Fund (LEAF) and working on the Indian Residential Schools Agreement.[98] In 2016, she issued the first judicial approval for an assisted death.

---

96   ibid.

97   Bryden, "Sources."

98   "Sheilah Martin," Wikipedia, *https://en.wikipedia.org/wiki/Sheilah_Martin.*

Interestingly, news of the disagreement between Trudeau and Wilson-Raybould over the Joyal recommendation appears not to have been leaked by sources close to Wilson-Raybould but by Trudeau's people. They evidently saw it as an opportunity to make it look like Wilson-Raybould was demoted from justice minister and attorney general over that, rather than over her refusal to play along with the corruption of the justice system in the SNC-Lavalin affair. The fingerprints of Trudeau's people were all over the version of the story that had been leaked to CTV, at the same time it was being leaked to the Canadian Press, when CTV's Glen McGregor reported that, "Trudeau was concerned that Joyal wasn't committed to protecting rights that have flown out of interpretation of the Charter of Rights and Freedoms, particularly LGBTQ2 rights and even abortion access, neither of which are specifically enshrined in the Charter" and that it had "caused Trudeau to question his justice minister's judgment."[99] Yet, as the National Post reported, "Joyal doesn't ever seem to have articulated a personal position on abortion," and it could not find "a word he's said about same-sex marriage in any context."[100]

Joyal recognized immediately that his good name and career was being dragged through the mud as a way for someone to discredit Wilson-Raybould, and issued a statement expressing his indignation.[101] "I fear that someone is using my previous candidacy to the Supreme Court of Canada to further an agenda unrelated to the appointment process," Joyal said. "This is wrong." Bar associations across the country spoke

99   Glen McGregor, "Relations between Trudeau, Wilson-Raybould began to fray over her Supreme Court pick: Sources," CTV News, March 25, 2019, *https:// www.ctvnews.ca/politics/relations-between-trudeau-wilson-raybould-began-to-fray-over-her-supreme-court-pick-sources-1.4350875.*

100   Chris Selley, "Trudeau Liberals—and the Anonymous Sources—hit rock bottom," *National Post*, March 26, 2019, *https://nationalpost.com/opinion/chris-selley-trudeau-liberals-and-the-anonymous-sources-hit-rock-bottom.*

101   Steven Chase and Robert Fife, "Chief Justice Glenn Joyal says his name's being used as part of 'agenda' in Jody Wilson-Raybould and Liberal dispute," *The Globe and Mail*, March 25, 2019, *https://www.theglobeandmail.com/canada/article-chief-justice-glenn-joyal-says-his-names-being-used-as-part-of/.*

out to denounce the breach of confidentiality in the judicial selection process.[102]

The Manitoba Bar Association issued a particularly blistering rebuke of the prime minister's sleazy smear campaign. "The recent breaches of confidentiality where the suitability of other candidates are discussed is highly disconcerting. It demeans the entire selection process and is harmful to the privacy of individual applicants," wrote Bar Association president Mark Toews in the statement. "The implication was given that Chief Justice Joyal could give rulings that would undermine the rights of women and members of the LGBTQ2S community. Such a suggestion is entirely improper, and indeed false. ... He has also defended the importance of protecting equality in society, as well as individual and group rights. Nothing in what he has done throughout his judicial career, nor in the publicized comments he has made, could suggest that he is against a woman's right to choose, same-sex marriage, or LGBTQ2S rights generally. It is most appalling that such an inaccurate description has been suggested or implied."

As if Trudeau cared about smearing a good non-Liberal judge or compromising the very judicial selection process he claimed he was committed to improving. In fact, that was just the beginning of his campaign to corrupt the judicial review process, and the justice system generally, as a way to entrench Liberal power and influence. Just a few weeks later, The Globe and Mail revealed that the prime minister's office hadn't just been vetoing Supreme Court judges for wrongthink, it was vetting all lower-court judicial appointment through a Liberal donor database called Liberalist, to identify and confirm party loyalists.[103] That's a list kept by the party ostensibly for election campaigns to identify Liberal voters, by keeping records of those who donate to the Liberal Party, have been members of the Liberal Party and who have participated in Liberal Party events. Only under the Trudeau

---

102   Jesse Ferreras, "Most appalling': Manitoba Bar Association blasts reports about Wilson-Raybould's Supreme Court pick," Global News, March 26, 2019, *https://globalnews.ca/news/5100221/manitoba-bar-association-glenn-joyal.*

103   Daniel Leblanc and Tom Cardoso, "PMO vets potential judges with private Liberal database," *The Globe and Mail*, April 24, 2019, *https://www.theglobeandmail.com/politics/article-pmo-vets-potential-judges-with-liberal-database/.*

government, it was being used as a test of loyalty and purity to screen potential judges. After all, they certainly wouldn't want another Glenn Joyal slipping through.

Finally the entire sham that was the supposedly independent judicial selection process was exposed for the fiction that it was. The Liberals' promise of a process that would promote "openness, transparency, accountability and diversity of Canada's judiciary" was incinerated on the revelation of blunt, naked partisan machinations.[104] Judicial appointments were, as they had been under Liberal governments in the past, once again available at the price of Liberal donations. Sure, the PMO had agreed to review the shortlists put out by the various judicial advisory committees (JACs). "However," the *Globe* reported, "sources said the process still includes a role for the PMO in vetting candidates further. The records show the PMO used Liberalist to evaluate candidates who had gone through the JAC process."

As just one example: two lawyers vetted in 2018 for possible appointments were given high marks as "supporters" of the Liberal party after their names were run through the Liberalist, which shows the years they were party members and "their history of donations to the party at the riding and national levels" and the fact they voted in the 2013 leadership race. The PMO eventually confirmed it was using the practice, but a spokesman for the attorney general still had the gall to say that, "All judicial appointments are made on the basis of merit." Yeah, right. Now we know what they meant all along by "meritorious." Under Trudeau, a staunch loyalty to the party is what makes judges "meritorious." You know, just like how they appoint judges in communist China.

In fact, the list of 289 judges appointed by the Trudeau government since 2016 revealed that there were four appointed who were Liberal

---

104   Department of Justice, "Government of Canada announces judicial appointments and reforms the appointments process to increase openness and transparency," press release, Oct. 20, 2016, *https://www.canada.ca/en/department-justice/news/2016/10/government-canada-announces-judicial-appointments-reforms-appointments-process-increase-openness-transparency.html.*

members, supporters and donors for every one appointed who had donated instead to the Conservatives or New Democrats. But that only tells part of the story: It's the difference in the size of the party donations that is truly staggering. Of all the donations made by judges appointed during that period, more than 90 per cent of the cash was given to the Liberal party, compared to less than five per cent each for the Conservative, NDP and Green parties.

But giving money to Liberals is just one way to secure a judgeship. Another is being cosy with Dominic LeBlanc, the powerful and influential friend, confidante and former babysitter of the prime minister. You see, being part of LeBlanc's family doesn't just put someone first in line for lucrative multi-million-dollar fishing licences arranged through an illegitimate expropriation of someone else's property justified by fake "reconciliation" claims. If you happen to be a lawyer, it also puts you in line for a plum appointment to the judicial bench.

That's what CBC New Brunswick discovered in July 2019, just weeks after the Liberalist judge scandal and just over three months since the PMO had been caught in a smear campaign to trash a respected judge so it could attack a political enemy.[105] Of the six most recent appointments to the bench in New Brunswick, an astonishing five of them had "strong connections" to LeBlanc. They included the wife of LeBlanc's brother-in-law, LeBlanc's neighbour at his summer house, and three lawyers who helped pay off the debt LeBlanc had accrued in his failed run for the federal party leadership in 2008. One of the appointments, Saint John lawyer Arthur T. Doyle, does not live anywhere near LeBlanc's riding, but has been a regular donor to LeBlanc's Beauséjour riding association. Clearly his strategic long-distance donating paid off. Marie-Claude Belanger-Richard is also a judge in Saint John, more than an hour's drive away from LeBlanc's riding. But she happens to be married to LeBlanc's brother-in-law. Moncton lawyer Robert M. Dysart and Boyle both gave money to

---

105   Jones, "Domenic."

retire LeBlanc's $31,000 leadership debt.[106] But all of that is just an overly detailed and unnecessarily complicated way of describing what the Liberals would simply call "meritorious."

---

106   ibid.

CHAPTER 5

THE MANY BRIBES OF SNC-LAVALIN

On August 5, 2016, as the Trudeau Liberals were just heading toward the close of their first year in government, they received a letter from the commissioner of Canada elections marked "confidential." It was a bombshell. The office of the commissioner is supposed to be the independent watchdog in charge of investigating violations of Canada's election laws. And the letter revealed one doozy of a violation.

It revealed that from the years 2004 to 2009, the Montreal-headquartered engineering and construction giant SNC-Lavalin had been running an illegal donation scheme to funnel money to the federal Liberal Party.[107] SNC-Lavalin had already earned a global reputation as a corrupt organization, having been caught in illegal bribery schemes in Mozambique, Uganda, Bangladesh and, most famously, Libya, to win

---

107   Harvey Cashore and Frédéric Zalac, "Names of SNC employees, executives behind thousands of dollars in illegal Liberal Party donations revealed," The Fifth Estate, CBC, April 30, 2019, *https://www.cbc.ca/news/politics/snc-lavalin-liberal-donors-list-canada-elections-1.5114537.*

juicy contracts from corrupt officials and governments.[108] In Canada, it had been caught in a multi-million-dollar bribery scheme to fix a deal so it could win a rich government contract to build and maintain the McGill University Health Centre — a contract it continues to profit from at taxpayers' expense, even today. In fact, SNC-Lavalin's nefariously obtained $1.3-billion contract ensures taxpayers keep shelling out millions of dollars a year to the company to maintain the health centre until 2044.[109]

And as company executives were rampantly bribing corrupt officials here and abroad, they were also making sure they cut the Liberals in on the action, by funnelling some of their money to the Libranos family. The commissioner's letter detailed how 18 former SNC-Lavalin employees, directors and even their spouses had written cheques to the federal Liberal Party disguised as personal donations. In reality, they were being funded by SNC-Lavalin itself, in violation of federal contribution limits. For every donation that employees made, former employees eventually revealed to the CBC, SNC-Lavalin would later award them a "bonus" worth twice as much. The Liberals raked in $110,000 in illegal donations. The same scheme, incidentally, sent a few bucks to the Conservative Party: $8,000, a small sum in comparison. SNC-Lavalin clearly had a very strong preference as to which party it wanted to see running the Canadian federal government.[110]

For a corrupt company to bet so heavily on the Liberals might have begun to look like a problem when the Trudeau Liberals unveiled their 2015 election platform. After all, they had promised to crack down on election fraud and to toughen up the independence of the elections

---

108   Jack Mintz, "Trudeau going soft on SNC-Lavalin's corruption could cost Canada a lot," *Financial Post*, March 15, 2019, *https://business.financialpost.com/opinion/jack-mintz-trudeau-going-soft-on-snc-lavalins-corruption-could-cost-canada-a-lot.*

109   "A closer look at SNC-Lavalin's sometimes murky past," CBC News, Feb. 8. 2019, *https://www.cbc.ca/news/canada/snc-lavalin-corruption-fraud-bribery-libya-muhc-1.5010865.*

110   Cashore and Zalac, "Names."

commissioner.[111] But SNC-Lavalin had bigger fish to fry to bother worrying about some illegal campaign contributions to their friends in the Liberal Party. The company was facing a criminal trial over the bribery and corruption it had engaged in in Libya. The Conservatives under Stephen Harper had shown a no-nonsense approach to corruption as they worked to wash the grime off the Canadian government left behind by the Liberals sponsorship scandal.[112] To get out of its legal jam, SNC-Lavalin needed a government that was far more open to corrupt nonsense.

And the Liberals immediately proved they were. While the elections commissioner had notified them of SNC-Lavalin's illegal donation scheme in August 2016, the Liberal Party sat on the letter for three years. So did Elections Canada. They kept it absolutely under wraps — totally hush-hush.[113] The signal to SNC-Lavalin couldn't have been clearer that the Liberals didn't mean a word they were saying in public about getting tougher on election corruption and the increased independence of the elections office. The Libranos were back and their corrupt friends would be well taken care of.

The elections commissioner would remarkably end up making a jaw-dropping deal with SNC-Lavalin. All that would happen is that the parties would refund the illegal money to SNC-Lavalin. It was the opposite of a punishment or a fine: The company actually got its money back. At least the Conservatives when asked by the CBC immediately agreed to make available the list of the malefactors who had given them the dirty donations, exposing them to some public embarrassment.[114] The Liberals, however, refused to cough up the names despite repeated requests from reporters. They were resolutely protecting their friends. And then, to top it all off, amazingly, Elections Canada agreed not to

---

111   Trudeau Meter, *https://trudeaumetre.polimeter.org/.*

112   Tristin Hopper, "The Harper government passed a measure 13 years ago to catch Liberal scandals. It worked perfectly," *National Post*, March 1, 2019, *https:// nationalpost.com/news/politics/the-tories-passed-a-measure-designed-to-catch-liberal-scandals-thirteen-years-later-it-caught-lavscam.*

113   Cashore and Zalac, "Names."

114   ibid.

prosecute the Liberal-friendly firm if it simply promised not to break the law again.[115] That was it. Imagine anyone else in Canada getting that kind of deal after being caught red-handed breaking a law that was integral to our society. Getting away with promising not to do it again. Oh, and getting your corrupt payments refunded back to you. What a deal for SNC-Lavalin: They further entrenched the loyalty and affection of the Liberal Party, without it ultimately costing them a cent.

That's not the kind of deal Canada's elections watchdogs have seen fit to offer Conservatives. Evidently, that's the kind of sweetheart deal only available to companies with a long, sordid and well-known history of corrupting governments worldwide. Dean Del Mastro was charged by the regulators at Elections Canada after running for re-election as a Tory MP in the 2008 election over violations of election rules by spending more of his own money on his campaign than was allowed by law (he was ejected from the Conservative caucus as soon as he was charged).[116] It wasn't that much money, all told: Del Mastro had written a personal cheque to Ottawa-based polling firm Hollinshed Research Group, without being reimbursed by donors, and didn't report it; if he had reported it, he would have been several thousand dollars over his strict personal contribution limit of $2,100. Not a lot of money either way — the illegal sum amounted to less than $20,000 — but it was clearly against the rules.[117]

Of course, an infraction representing a wrongful donation of less than $20,000 is a lot less than what SNC-Lavalin was caught doing, with $110,000 illegally funnelled to the Liberals. Del Mastro was found criminally guilty for violating the Elections Act and sentenced to prison — into an actual prison cell — for a month. He was literally led

---

115   ibid.

116   Stephen Maher, "Del Mastro trial now awaits closing arguments," *Ottawa Citizen*, July 16, 2014, *https://ottawacitizen.com/news/national/campaign-workers-knew-nothing-about-voter-contact-firm-del-mastro-trial-told*.

117   Steven Chase, "Tory MP Dean Del Mastro resigns from caucus, stripped of Parliamentary Secretary job," *The Globe and Mail*, Sept. 26, 2013, *https://www.theglobeandmail.com/news/politics/tory-mp-dean-del-mastro-charged-by-elections-canada-with-concealing-21000/article14547903/*.

out of the court in leg irons and handcuffs to do hard time.[118] Then he had to serve another four months of house arrest. The judge said in her ruling that violating the three rules he was convicted for breaking — exceeding spending limits; failing to report a personal contribution; and knowingly submitting a false document — constituted "cheating and lying" that represented an "affront" to the principles of Canadian democracy. She called it the "antithesis" of democracy.[119] She said that they needed to be punished with "serious sanctions" including jail time "to reflect the need for denunciation and deterrence." She was, in other words, throwing the book at him to make an example of him.

But hold on a minute. If one Conservative MP's illegal contributions worth less than $20,000 are the "antithesis" of democracy and an "affront" to Canada's democratic principles that require severe "denunciation and deterrence," then where does that put the more than $100,000 in illegal contributions by the Liberals' corrupt friends at SNC-Lavalin? The Liberals' sleazy cronies schemed to line the party's pockets with six times more in illicit corporate cash than Del Mastro had shelled out from his own pocket, to donate to his own campaign. Del Mastro broke the rules, sure. He should face consequence for it. But it's important to note that he wasn't trying to bribe anyone. He wasn't stealing money from unknowing shareholders and funnelling it to buy influence with a political party well-known for corruption scandals, including the notorious Adscam, which was all about dirty money being secretly funnelled between unscrupulous Quebec firms and the Liberal Party. Del Mastro spent a bit too much of his own personal money — rather than using donors' money for the same purpose, which could have been perfectly fine in the eyes of the law — on trying to win re-election to his former seat.

---

118   "Convicted MP Del Mastro in leg irons for jail transport standard procedure: OPP," Canadian Press, June 27, 2015, *https://www.advocatedaily.com/ convicted-mp-del-mastro-in-leg-irons-for-jail-transport-standard-procedure-opp.html*.

119   "Dean Del Mastro sentenced to month in jail, 4 months house arrest for election overspending," CBC News, June 25, 2015, *https://www.cbc.ca/news/ politics/dean-del-mastro-sentenced-to-month-in-jail-4-months-house-arrest-for-election-overspending-1.3126992*.

Obviously, there is a big difference between what he did and what SNC-Lavalin did. The folks at the election commissioner's office certainly saw a big difference. To them, the difference was obvious: Del Mastro was running for the Conservative Party, so what he did must be prosecuted as a criminal and punished to the fullest extent of the law. The money launderers at SNC-Lavalin were only trying to help the Liberals, so they could be let off with a warning and a so-called "compliance agreement" agreeing not to do it again Then the election commissioner and Elections Canada would just quietly keep the matter under wraps from the public for years, secretly telling only the Liberal Party that had struck the shady deal, and the party would help keep it all covered up. Hey, who says the public needs to know about an "affront" to democracy that undermines the integrity of our system, when it involves the Liberals, after all? It took reporters to dig the whole story out and bring it to light.

The appalling hypocrisy of the commissioner of Canada elections wasn't lost on Del Mastro, who said it was a clear sign that there needed to be far more transparency around the agency, given such a glaring bias.[120] "This is an agency with tremendous power and authority. It has tremendous responsibilities and it seems to be using those powers and those abilities to prosecute those that it doesn't like and to protect those that it seems to like and that's quite disturbing," said Del Mastro in May 2019 after the illegal Liberal donation scheme was finally revealed. "If, for example, a compliance agreement is appropriate in this matter then why wasn't it appropriate in other matters when the Commissioner of Canada Elections decided to go ahead and press charges on what I would argue were much, much lesser situations?"[121]

The sordid deal that arranged for SNC-Lavalin to secure a "compliance agreement" and the secret scheme covered up for years by the Liberals with the help of friendly leading bureaucrats in the civil service was a striking foreshadow of more squalid hush-hush dealings to come

---

120   Tyler Buist, "Former Tory MP Del Mastro, convicted of electoral offences in 2015, coming to Ottawa in push for transparency," CBC News, May 7, 2019, *https://www.cbc.ca/news/politics/powerandpolitics/del-mastro-transparency-push-1.5127088.*

121   ibid.

between the corrupt Quebec company and the easily corrupted federal party. That kind of under-the-table, seedy, get-out-of-jail deal between SNC-Lavalin and the government was exactly what the Liberals had been conspiring to arrange in getting their corrupt Quebec pals off the hook for even more serious infractions — these ones involving charges of bribery and corruption as it eagerly cozied up to become best friends with one of the Middle East's most grotesque dictatorships.[122]

---

122   Robert Fife, Steven Chase and Sean Fine, "PMO pressed Wilson-Raybould to abandon prosecution of SNC-Lavalin; Trudeau denies his office 'directed' her" *The Globe and Mail*, Feb. 7, 2019, *https://www.theglobeandmail.com/politics/article-pmo-pressed-justice-minister-to-abandon-prosecution-of-snc-lavalin/.*

CHAPTER 6

CANADA'S MOST CORRUPT COMPANY FALLS IN LOVE WITH TRUDEAU

SNC-Lavalin had never thought it should pay a price for its dirty behaviour, whether it was illegal donations to the Liberal Party — or worse. Why should it? It was a corporate jewel in the crown of "Quebec Inc.", one of the most politically pampered and protected business sectors in the country, where corruption and collusion were merely winked at as part of the culture.[123]

The history of business in the province featured a "a long line of made-in-Quebec corruption that has affected the province's political culture at every level," as *Maclean's* put it in a 2010 cover story. The famous stories that revealed alleged construction rackets involving the mafia and the Hells Angels running the construction arm of the largest labour union in Quebec, the mayor of Montreal being arrested for bribery,

---

123   Martin Patriquin, "Quebec: The most corrupt province," *Maclean's*, Sept. 24, 2010, *https://www.macleans.ca/news/canada/the-most-corrupt-province/*.

and of course Adscam, were just the tip of the iceberg.[124, 125] There were countless stories of criminality involving Quebec businesses and dirty politicians that no one ever found out about, and probably never would.

By the time Trudeau was taking over as leader of the Liberal Party and heading to his 2015 election victory, SNC-Lavalin was surely fed up with having uncooperative watchdogs outside its home province stubbornly refusing to tolerate its criminality. The Asian Development Bank had disbarred SNC from its contracts in 2004 over the company's corrupt practices.[126] The World Bank had banned the company in 2013 for the same reason. And the previous Conservative government right here in Canada had broken with the long tradition of turning a blind eye to the malfeasance of Quebec firms by having the temerity to pass tough anti-corruption measures, including a rule that would make it possible for firms charged with criminal activity here or in foreign countries to be banned from bidding on federal government contracts for up to 10 years.[127]

Then, even worse for the company, under the Harper government, the RCMP and federal prosecutors actually had the gall to charge SNC-Lavalin with corruption and fraud over alleged bribes it had given to top members of the regime of Moammar Gadhafi to secure

---

124   "Hells Angels, Mob ran FTQ construction wing, witness says," CBC News, Oct. 2, 2013, *https://www.cbc.ca/news/canada/montreal/hells-angels-mob-ran-ftq-construction-wing-witness-says-1.1876930.*

125   Jaela Bernstien and Benjamin Shingler, "Ex-Montreal mayor Michael Applebaum found guilty of corruption," CBC News, *https://www.cbc.ca/news/canada/montreal/applebaum-ruling-corruption-1.3952413.*

126   Jack Mintz, "Trudeau going soft on SNC-Lavalin's corruption could cost Canada a lot," *Financial Post*, March 15, 2019, *https://business.financialpost.com/opinion/jack-mintz-trudeau-going-soft-on-snc-lavalins-corruption-could-cost-canada-a-lot.*

127   Terence Corcoran, "Canada's real corruption scandal: How Ottawa bungled a flawed OECD code and triggered the SNC crisis," *Financial Post*, March 15, 2019, *https://business.financialpost.com/news/fp-street/canadas-real-corruption-scandal-how-ottawa-bungled-a-flawed-oecd-anti-bribery-code-and-triggered-the-snc-crisis.*

construction deals being handed out by the Libyan dictator and his family.[128] SNC-Lavalin executives had paid $160 million in bribes to Gadhafi's son, Saadi, in exchange for billions of dollars' worth of engineering contracts, including building an airport, the largest-manmade irrigation project on earth (called the Great Man-Made River) and, most fittingly, a prison.[129]

That would have been a prison like Abu Salim, in Tripoli, Libya, where in 1996, the Gadhafi regime massacred what Human Rights Watch estimates was nearly 1,300 prisoners after they dared to protest "restricted family visits and poor living conditions."[130] No one knows the exact number of those killed, of course, because many prisoners under the Gadhafi regime were kidnapped secretly and held in prison without anyone knowing there actual whereabouts, and because after the massacre, the bodies were seen being thrown into a mass grave that was then filled with cement.[131] Survivors were too fearful of retribution to talk about it, investigators later reported.

In Libya, that would likely be the kind of prison where political prisoners of the notoriously tyrannical Gadhafi regime were kept. The government, which was tightly controlled by Gadhafi and his sons, were famous for decades of human rights abuses, with horrific allegations of state-sanctioned rape, torture, kidnapping, extrajudicial executions of political enemies, secret imprisonment and murder for anyone that

---

128   Bertrand Marotte, "RCMP charges SNC-Lavalin with bribery, fraud," *The Globe and Mail*, Feb. 19, 2015, *https://www.theglobeandmail.com/report-on-business/rcmp-charges-snc-lavalin-with-bribery-fraud/article23070193/*.

129   ibid.

130   Human Rights Watch, "Libya: June 1996 Killings at Abu Salim Prison," June 27, 2006, *https://www.hrw.org/news/2006/06/27/libya-june-1996-killings-abu-salim-prison*.

131   ibid.

the dictator and his family chose to target.[132, 133] There were stories of Gadhafi having teenage girls kidnapped from local schools — some schoolgirls as young as 14 — and imprisoned in "sex dungeons" for his personal sadistic pleasure and abuse.

The Gadhafi regime was also behind the bombing of Pan Am Flight 103 flying to New York from London, over Lockerbie, Scotland, that killed 270 people.[134] It was the first mass-killing of Americans by terrorists in history, and the worst to happen until 9/11, and the two perpetrators were actual intelligence officers working for the Gadhafi regime.[135]

These were the monsters that SNC-Lavalin was eager to work with.

In fact, SNC-Lavalin wasn't just happy to work with the Gadhafis; the company grew exceptionally cosy with them. The RCMP found evidence that SNC-Lavalin execs had bought luxury yachts as gifts for their friend Saadi Gadhafi. "One of the boats, the Hokulani, is a 45-metre superyacht with two VIP suites, a Jacuzzi, an entertainment room with a flat screen TV and accommodation for 10," reported the National Post as the evidence was revealed in 2013.[136] SNC-Lavalin paid to redecorate a condo in Toronto for their friend Saadi to use as a

---

132   "Factbox: Gaddafi rule marked by abuses, rights groups say," Reuters, Feb. 22, 2011, *https://www.reuters.com/article/us-libya-protest-abuses/factbox-gaddafi-rule-marked-by-abuses-rights-groups-say-idUSTRE71L1NH20110222.*

133   "Gruesome Details of Gadhafi's Rape of Teenagers and Other Crimes Revealed," *Ha'aretz*, Jan. 26, 2014, *https://www.haaretz.com/gadhafi-s-crimes-revealed-1.5315653.*

134   Wikipedia, "Pan Am Flight 103," *https://en.wikipedia.org/wiki/Pan_Am_Flight_103.*

135   Garrett M. Graff, "Pan Am Flight 103: Robert Mueller's 30-Year Search for Justice," *Wired*, Dec. 27, 2018, *https://www.wired.com/story/robert-muellers-search-for-justice-for-pan-am-103/.*

136   Stewart Bell, "Millions in SNC-Lavalin bribes bought Gaddafi's playboy son luxury yachts, unsealed RCMP documents allege," *National Post*, Jan. 25, 2013, *https://nationalpost.com/news/millions-in-snc-lavalin-bribes-bought-gaddafi-son-luxury-yachts-unsealed-rcmp-documents-allege.*

party pad as he travelled to Canada.[137] The Quebec firm hired personal bodyguards for Saadi when he was travelling here. They even allegedly paid tens of thousands of dollars to buy him prostitutes.[138] When one bodyguard company refused to be party to securing prostitutes for him, SNC-Lavalin gave the contract to another firm instead.

Then, in an even more astonishing move, SNC-Lavalin allegedly tried to smuggle its pal Saadi out of Libya as his father's regime was being toppled.[139] As NATO-backed Libyan rebels uprising against the Gadhafi regime were in the process of fighting to overthrow their longtime oppressors in a 2011 civil war, the dictator-supporting brass at SNC-Lavalin were working to help ensure at least one of those oppressors found a safe haven in Mexico by arranging to have him secretly transported there.[140] The audacious plot didn't end up working in the end: Saadi ended up fleeing to Niger. But think about that: The Gadhafis weren't even in power anymore. They almost certainly never would be again. Saadi's brother, Saif, would be captured by militia troops.[141] His father was being hunted by the rebels who would soon find and kill him.[142] And yet so personally chummy was SNC-Lavalin with these reprehensible creeps, these rapists and mass murderers, these

---

137   Stewart Bell, "The Gaddafi condo: Redecorated at SNC-Lavalin's expense, luxury Toronto suite sits unused amid UN inaction," Global News, March 14, 2019, *https://globalnews.ca/news/5030733/saadi-gaddafis-toronto-condo/*.

138   Marie-Danielle Smith, "SNC-Lavalin paid for Gadhafi son's debauchery while he was in Canada: report," *National Post*, Feb. 27, 2019, *https://nationalpost. com/news/politics/snc-lavalin-paid-for-gadhafi-sons-debauchery-while-he-was-in-canada-report*.

139   ibid.

140   "How the Post revealed the failed plot to smuggle Saadi Gaddafi into Mexico," *National Post*, Dec. 8, 2011, *https://nationalpost.com/news/canada/how-the-post-revealed-the-failed-plot-to-smuggle-saadi-gaddafi-into-mexico*.

141   Chris Stephen and David Batty, "Saif al-Islam Gaddafi captured in Libya," *The Guardian*, Nov. 19, 2011, *https://www.theguardian.com/world/2011/nov/19/saif-al-islam-gaddafi-captured*.

142   Peter Beaumont and Chris Stephen, "Gadaffi's last words as he begged for mercy: 'What did I do to you?'," *The Guardian*, Oct. 23, 2011, *https://www. theguardian.com/world/2011/oct/23/gaddafi-last-words-begged-mercy*.

sponsors of terror, that the company was still pulling out all the stops to help a Gadhafi brother out, even as the dictatorship was finished.

And this is the company that the Liberals are best pals with. SNC-Lavalin had never thought it should pay a price for its dirty behaviour, and the Libranos, under Justin Trudeau, couldn't agree more.

In fact, look at it from Trudeau's point of view: hadn't SNC-Lavalin shown tremendous loyalty? Hadn't they shown that they truly "get" him — the private jets, the luxury lifestyle, the secrecy? Far from disqualifying them, SNC-Lavalin's misconduct in Libya was exactly the kind of friends the king of the Libranos wanted to have for himself.

So, if SNC-Lavalin was in trouble, the Trudeau Liberals were going to stand by them to help the company out as much as they could, just like SNC-Lavalin had stood by the Gadhafis, through thick and thin. After all, it's not just any company that would be so loyal to the Liberals and so ethically flexible as to set up a kickback scheme within their corporate structure to funnel tens of thousands of dollars in illegal donations to the party.

And the Liberals, it turned out, were so loyal and ethically flexible themselves that they were willing to do far more than just help SNC-Lavalin cover up that very scheme, and permanently conceal the names of the perpetrators. They were willing to corrupt the very justice system to get SNC-Lavalin out of the criminal charges that had been brought against SNC-Lavalin under the Harper government.

SNC-Lavalin CEO Neil Bruce first approached the Liberals to call a favour in from his company's political chums in January 2018, on the sidelines of the Davos, Switzerland World Economic Forum, famous as the annual insufferable gathering of elitist, globalist grandees. Naturally, Bruce knew he'd find Trudeau and his people there. In fact, Trudeau would be giving one of his trademark self-congratulatory speeches, touting his crusade to end gender imbalances forever.[143] The bill to taxpayers for Trudeau travelling to hob-knob at a Swiss ski resort

---

143   "Justin Trudeau's Davos address in full," World Economic Forum, Jan. 23, 2018, *https://www.weforum.org/agenda/2018/01/pm-keynote-remarks-for-world-economic-forum-2018/*.

and feel that desperately-craved warm glow of approval from his fellow liberal elitists was a mere $700,000.[144] But Trudeau said it was worth it.[145] Of course he did.

Most importantly for Bruce, the Liberals had been in power just over two years by the time they had swanned into Davos, and by then had very clearly demonstrated their flagrant disregard for matters of government ethics and their blatant indifference to the law. Bruce had already tried working with the Conservative government in 2015, before the Liberals were elected, but the talks "reportedly stalled" and so "the company was waiting to see which party would form the next government" before trying again.[146] Luckily, after having gotten nowhere with the Harper Conservatives, who evidently felt no urge to let a corrupt company slide off the hook just for the heck of it, SNC-Lavalin caught just the break it was looking for in the October 2015 election.

By the time that Bruce caught up with members of Trudeau's team, including Finance Minister Bill Morneau, the prime minister had already been found to have broken federal law in arranging free trips to the billionaire's island getaway belonging to the Aga Khan, along with fellow Liberal Seamus O'Regan, without disclosing it to the ethics

144   Laura Stone, "Trudeau government's Davos trip cost taxpayers nearly $700,000: documents," *The Globe and Mail*, April 2, 2018, *https://www. theglobeandmail.com/politics/article-trudeau-governments-davos-trip-cost-taxpayers-nearly-70000/*.

145   Karina Roman, "Trudeau defends cost of Davos trip, 'looks forward' to what Trump will say," CBC News, Jan. 25, 2018, *https://www.cbc.ca/news/politics/trudeau-davos-costs-trump-1.4503355*.

146   Mario Dion, *Trudeau II Report made under the Conflict of Interest Act*, Office of the Conflict of Interest and Ethics Commissioner, August 2019, *http://ciec-ccie.parl.gc.ca/Documents/English/Public%20Reports/Examination%20Reports/Trudeau%20II%20Report.pdf*.

commissioner.[147, 148] In fact, he had tried to conceal what amounted to an illegal gift solicited from a lobbyist —the Aga Khan — and then lied about his relationship with that lobbyist, as a way of trying to get out of trouble.

Also, by the time Bruce flew into Switzerland to cleverly arrange a most strategic "bumping into" with the Liberal finance minister, the Liberals had already learned from the Commissioner of Canada Elections that SNC-Lavalin had corrupted its own internal payroll processes and broken federal elections law all to arrange for six-figures' worth of extra donations to find their way into the Liberal war chest, right at a time when the party was trying to claw its way back to power and needed the money the most.[149]

And by the time Trudeau was accepting gifts of brightly patterned socks from his fellow Davos attendees that January, the Liberal Party had more than a year earlier cast its lot with the illegal behaviour of SNC-Lavalin by agreeing not to get tough on the firm for its illegal donation. Quite the opposite: it wanted to help conceal the company's criminal enterprise by helping it cover the whole scheme up.[150, 151]

And, while he was arranging his trip to Davos and the beginning of his company's conspiracy with the Liberals to get his company out of the criminal charges it had been saddled with under the previous

---

147   Mary Dawson, *The Trudeau Report made under the Conflict of Interest Act and Conflict of Interest Code for Members of the House of Commons*, Office of the Conflict of Interest and Ethics Commissioner, Dec. 20, 2017, *http://ciec-ccie. parl.gc.ca/Documents/English/Public%20Reports/Examination%20Reports/The%20 Trudeau%20Report.pdf.*

148   Marie-Danielle Smith, "Seamus O'Regan may face inquiry for failure to disclose Aga Khan vacation with PM to ethics commissioner," *National Post*, April 11, 2018, *https://nationalpost.com/news/politics/oregan-may-face-inquiry-for-failure-to-disclose-aga-khan-vacation-with-pm-to-ethics-commissioner.*

149   Harvey Cashore and Frédéric Zalac, "Names of SNC employees, executives behind thousands of dollars in illegal Liberal Party donations revealed," The Fifth Estate, CBC, April 30, 2019, *https://www.cbc.ca/news/politics/snc-lavalin-liberal-donors-list-canada-elections-1.5114537.*

150   Roman, "Trudeau."

151   Cashore and Zalac, "Names."

government, Bruce would have also been aware by then that the finance minister himself had been found to have his own challenges with following the law. Just a few months before their global-elite meet-cute, Bill Morneau was publicly outed for having failed to report to the ethics watchdog his millionaire's villa in the South of France, as required by law.[152] If there was anywhere that Thousand-Dollar-Bill Morneau was bound to find some sympathy over how hard it can be to keep track of all your vacation homes, Davos was surely the place.

So by the time the snows were falling in Switzerland on the world's richest thinkers and most photogenic politicians, Neil Bruce of SNC-Lavalin would have already had a pretty good idea of how easily the Trudeau Liberals could see their way past annoyingly democratic things like laws, and ethics, and transparency. He was already dealing with a government with a demonstrated eagerness to deceive, conceal, break the law and cover for its lawbreaking friends. And he would have had a really good idea of how eager the Liberals under Trudeau were to stay extra-special close friends with their corporate pals in Montreal working at the SNC-Lavalin headquarters. He knew, in other words, that in asking the Liberals' help in getting the company out of trouble for its recent history of gross corruption there would be nothing that would stand in the Liberals' way in doing him that favour. Not even the law.

And what was the favour Bruce wanted to ask? It was to get the Trudeau government's help in arranging for the company to not face charges for corruption and bribery. This was because — and this is so important to remember — a conviction would have made the company ineligible to bid on government contracts for the next five to 10 years.[153] Contracts that would be handed out, if things went according to plan, by a friendly Liberal government, presuming Trudeau were re-elected in 2019. And at the time Bruce began his campaign to win that favour,

---

152   Elizabeth Thompson, "Finance Minister Bill Morneau waited 2 years to disclose company that owns his French villa to ethics watchdog," Oct. 13, 2017, *https://www.cbc.ca/news/politics/morneau-company-france-ethics-1.4351933*.

153   Gabriel Friedman, "Here's how a new escape route could open up for SNC-Lavalin," *Financial Post*, Feb. 22, 2019, *https://business.financialpost.com/news/fp-street/heres-how-a-new-escape-route-could-open-up-for-snc-lavalin*.

in January 2018, there was no reason to think Trudeau wouldn't be. Polls back then had the Liberals soaring over their closest rivals, the Conservatives, with average polling projections on the day of the Davos meeting putting the Liberals at 39.5 per cent popularity, compared to 33.5 per cent for the Tories, and just 15.6 per cent for the NDP.[154]

That sounds like high stakes. And Bruce — and the Liberals — would go on to play a game so dirty, so underhanded and so unseemly, it was clear the stakes were critical. In fact — and again, this is terribly important — the ban almost certainly would not have been fatal for SNC-Lavalin. The company had already faced similar disbarments from bidding on contracts with the World Bank, because of the company's corrupt practices, in 2013.[155] It was disbarred for years from bidding on contracts for the Asian Development Bank, in 2004, over fraudulent company activities.[156] The company had weathered punishments for corruption before. The difference this time? It didn't think it should have to. Not now that their pals and co-conspirators, the Liberals, were in charge of things. This wasn't like the Asian Development Bank or the World Bank. This was Canada — the Libranos' home turf.

It should be noted, the costs of being disbarred were not, in the end, even particularly high. Not many people realize that SNC-Lavalin has, over the years, become more of a British company than a Canadian one. It has more workers based in the United Kingdom — 10,000 — than the 8,500 workers it has in Canada. Even Bruce himself is British. Before joining SNC-Lavalin just five years before the Davos meeting, in 2013, he was a top executive at the Scottish engineering

---

154 Canada Votes 2019 Poll Tracker, CBC, for Jan. 23, 2018, *https:// newsinteractives.cbc.ca/elections/poll-tracker/canada/.*

155 Mintz, "Trudeau."

156 ibid.

firm Amec.[157] He was made an officer of the Order of the British Empire in 2012.[158]

Of more than $9 billion in revenues that SNC-Lavalin earned the fiscal year that ended just before that fateful meeting between Bruce and Morneau in Davos, less than one-third were earned in Canada, and analysts estimated that about half of that was from federal government contracts.[159] So, maybe that's one-sixth of its massive, multi-billion business might be affected. Note — *they might be.* That is, if the prosecution against the company even succeeded. A prosecution relying on evidence linked to a deposed government, a dead dictator, his son hiding in Niger, with executives that had been let go from SNC-Lavalin years ago, and events that occurred years back, some as long ago as 2001. I wouldn't bet too much on the government's case standing up against SNC-Lavalin's cadre of top-notch, thousand-dollar-an-hour defence lawyers. Would you?

And note that the ban would not necessarily even have been for that long. Something else that not many people are aware of is that, if SNC-Lavalin were convicted, it could be disbarred from Canadian federal government contracts for up to 10 years — but that's only the maximum length of time. There are circumstances where the ban could be as short as five years.[160] In the meantime, shortly after the bribery and corruption charges were laid against SNC-Lavalin, the company signed an agreement with the government that allowed it to keep winning contracts, and adding jobs and profit at taxpayers'

157   Russell Lynch, "Neil Bruce: The Scottish engineer building an empire with SNC-Lavalin — and rebuilding damaged reputations," *Evening Standard,* July 14, 2017, *https://www.standard.co.uk/business/neil-bruce-the-scottish-engineer-building-an-empire-with-snclavalin-and-rebuilding-damaged-a3588101.html.*

158   Canadian Business Resource, "Executive Profiles: Mr. Neil Bruce," accessed Aug. 18, 2019, *http://www.cbr.ca/PersonProfile.aspx?PersonID=112764.*

159   "Here's what a 10-year ban on federal contract bids would mean for SNC-Lavalin," CBC News, March 7, 2019, *https://www.cbc.ca/news/business/financial-fall-out-snc-lavalin-1.5047742.*

160   Friedman, "Here's."

expense, even while it awaited trial.[161] So it's been business as usual since the charges were laid, anyway.

It would also later emerge that SNC-Lavalin had a "Plan B" if it couldn't weasel out of the prosecutions: It was willing to split its company into two, so as to have, so to speak, one "clean" company and one "dirty" one.[162] But even then, whatever work SNC-Lavalin was not doing for the federal government wouldn't necessarily be totally lost: It would have freed up capacity for the company to pursue other projects that it might have otherwise passed on.

Of course, that would mean hustling to win work fair-and-square from private investors, rather than the easier, sleazier route that SNC-Lavalin's executives still seem to prefer: Greasing the wheels of corruptible governments for profit.

---

161   SNC-Lavalin, "SNC-Lavalin signs an administrative agreement under the Government of Canada's new Integrity Regime," press release, Canada News Wire, Dec. 10, 2015, *https://www.newswire.ca/news-releases/snc-lavalin-signs-an-administrative-agreement-under-the-government-of-canadas-new-integrity-regime-561415391.html.*

162   "SNC-Lavalin executives ponder company break-up at private shareholder luncheon," *Financial Post*, May 7, 2019, *https://business.financialpost.com/news/fp-street/snc-lavalin-execs-ponder-company-break-up-at-private-shareholder-luncheon.*

CHAPTER 7

SNC-LAVALIN BUYS THE PRIME MINISTER'S OFFICE

As relatively low as the stakes were for SNC-Lavalin in facing prosecution over charges related to decades-old allegations involving a now-defunct government that maybe endangered at most a fraction of its business for a few years, the stakes were even lower for Canada.

The company might want you to think that its 8,500 jobs in Canada were at risk if it were banned from federal taxpayer contracts. It certainly wanted the Liberals to think that way. But again, something like an estimated half of its business in Canada was related to federal government contracts.[163] So that immediately means far fewer jobs would ever be at risk than the total SNC-Lavalin workforce in Canada. And even those jobs connected to government projects might not be necessarily lost: Surely many if not most of them are already working on government projects that SNC-Lavalin had already secured contracts

---

163   "Here's what a 10-year ban on federal contract bids would mean for SNC-Lavalin," CBC News, March 7, 2019, *https://www.cbc.ca/news/business/financial-fall-out-snc-lavalin-1.5047742.*

for. Those people would keep working on those projects. And as for those few employees whose work might wind up over the course of a few years of debarment, they might instead be assigned to new, non-government contracts won by SNC-Lavalin, assuming the company put in the actual effort to win some new business over the course of those years.

Even if, in the end, SNC-Lavalin had less work to do overall, other companies, its competitors, would be winning those contracts instead. It's not like the federal government would just stop giving out contracts if SNC-Lavalin were disbarred. It would simply award them to companies that had not been convicted of outrageous corruption. And so those companies would add whatever jobs might be lost at SNC-Lavalin. The economy would continue to function exactly the same way it had before. It's just that SNC-Lavalin would have to suffer a few years of consequences. The rest of Canada, however, would not.

So these were the miserably low stakes that SNC-Lavalin and the Trudeau government were playing for in what would become the most shocking political scandal since, well, the last time the Liberals in power. Actually, that's not quite true. The SNC-Lavalin scandal is even worse than the Adscam scandal. Adscam was gross, but at least it was a pretty basic corruption story that involved misspent government money, funnelled to the pockets of Liberal cronies to benefit the party in power. The SNC-Lavalin scandal was the Liberals' attempt to pervert the entire Canadian justice system to do special favours for an alleged criminal organization. It wasn't about just greasy cash. It was about undermining our hard-won system of law and order. It was a strike at democracy itself.

On August 14, 2019, the report on the SNC-Lavalin scandal by Conflict of Interest and Ethics Commissioner Mario Dion landed on Parliament Hill with all the mess and stench of a dead and decaying moose hoisted on the prime minister's doorstep. The report was simply called *Trudeau II made under the Conflict of Interest Act.*[164] That title alone is amazing, isn't it? *Trudeau II.* The sequel. The new Libranos boss had been in power less than one term, less than four years, and he was already on his *second* conflict of interest and ethics investigation! And just like the last one, which exposed his deceit, his self-interest and his disregard for the law when he solicited and accepted invaluable gifts from the Aga Khan, a registered lobbyist, this one would reach the same damning conclusion. Prime Minister Justin Trudeau had broken the law. Again. For the second time in less than four years.

The report laid out in graphic and grotesque detail just how serious this scandal is. It raises the level of the SNC-Lavalin affair from the "merely unlawful to the potentially criminal," as Postmedia columnist Andrew Coyne remarked upon its release.[165]

The first amazing detail revealed by Dion is how SNC-Lavalin was able to essentially direct the Liberals to do what it wanted in order to execute its own company strategy to get itself out of criminal charges. It needed what was called a deferred-prosecution agreement (DPA), also known as a remediation agreement. Up until late 2018, Canada's Criminal Code didn't have one; some other countries did. The DPA is a kind of plea bargain that would allow the company to admit wrongdoing and pay a fine, with a promise to never break the law again, as a way of putting a stop to the prosecution against it. Once all the terms were considered fulfilled, the charges could be dropped.[166] But if the company broke any of its promises before then, then the

---

164   Mario Dion, *Trudeau II Report made under the Conflict of Interest Act,* Office of the Conflict of Interest and Ethics Commissioner, August 2019, *http:// ciec-ccie.parl.gc.ca/Documents/English/Public%20Reports/Examination%20Reports/ Trudeau%20II%20Report.pdf.*

165   Andrew Coyne, "The deception in the SNC affair is the most troubling aspect of all," National Post, Aug. 16, 2019, *https://nationalpost.com/opinion/andrew-coyne-the-deception-in-the-snc-affair-is-the-most-troubling-aspect-of-all.*

166   Lawrence E. Ritchie and Malcolm Aboud, "Deferred Prosecution Agreements (DPAs) come into force in Canada," Osler, Risk Management and Crisis Response Blog, Sept. 19, 2018, *https://www.osler.com/en/blogs/risk/september-2018/ deferred-prosecution-agreements-dpas-come-into-force-in-canada.*

prosecution could always be restarted — you know, years and years later, when the case would stand even less of a chance of succeeding.

SNC-Lavalin desperately wanted a way out of its charges through the use of a DPA. But, remember, Canada didn't have DPAs in early 2018, when the company's CEO Neil Bruce met with Finance Minister Bill Morneau and his people in Davos, Switzerland at the World Economic Forum. Bruce's first step, then, was to get the Liberals to create one in the Criminal Code — and then give one to SNC-Lavalin.[167]

Think about that. SNC-Lavalin couldn't abide by Canadian law, evidently. So it actually wanted to change the law to suit itself. It literally wanted the government to change the punishments for certain crimes, *after it had already been charged with committing the crime*! Imagine that in any other circumstance. Imagine if a powerful businessman had been caught sexually assaulting his secretary and he then tried to persuade the government to change the penalty for sexual assault to allow him to apologize, pay a fine and promise never to do it again. That would be laughable. It would be an insult to the very rule of law we have in Canada. Yet not only did SNC-Lavalin think it could get away with trying to persuade the government that the punishment for a crime it had already been charged should be lightened — just for its own benefit. It actually *persuaded the government to do just that*!

Now, to be fair, let's put ourselves in Neil Bruce's shoes here. First of all, the CEO does have a fiduciary duty to his shareholders to save the company from as much punishment as he can. That's why Bruce was hired, after all; he was promoted to CEO of SNC-Lavalin in 2015 (having been hired two years earlier to run its oil and gas division).[168] By then, the company fully understood the legal mess it had put itself in. Bruce was supposed to help get it out.

---

167   Dion, *Trudeau II.*

168   Gabriel Friedman, "SNC-Lavalin CEO Neil Bruce in the spotlight as 'reputational hits' keep coming for embattled company," Financial Post, May 2, 2019,   *https://business.financialpost.com/commodities/snc-lavalin-ceo-neil-bruce-in-the-spotlight-as-reputational-hits-keep-coming-for-embattled-company.*

But remember, also that the following year, in 2016, the company had tested the Liberals' willingness to overlook its illegal activities — and found them more than happy to do so. It was in August that year that the Liberals had been informed that SNC-Lavalin had made six-figures' worth of illegal donations, almost all of it to the federal Liberal Party.[169] And the Liberals' response? They covered the whole thing up. They didn't tell a soul. And the punishment feebly handled out by the government's supposed elections watchdogs? That SNC-Lavalin got all its illegally donated money back — and had to promise never to do it again.

That's exactly the kind of punishment-free apology that the company was looking for in getting its hands on a DPA. You can't blame Neil Bruce for expecting it. He couldn't get it under the Harper Conservatives. But after waiting that out, and then witnessing his company's experience with the illegal-donations test, he would have only naturally figured this was the way things were done in Liberal Canada.

And here's the most incredible part about that: *He was right!*

As Dion details in his report, the meeting between Bruce and Bill Morneau and Liberal staffers in Davos only planted the seed that Canada needed a DPA for corrupt companies who were really, very sorry. It planted it very firmly. But just a few days later, the company delivered to Morneau's policy director, Justin To, "a confidential discussion document outlining reasons in support of a remediation agreement regime and the company's request for timely implementation of a regime via the federal budget."[170]

Look at that: SNC-Lavalin wasn't just saying it needed a DPA, also known as a remediation agreement. It was telling the government *how quickly* it should get it done, and *how* it should get it done, by passing it

---

169   Harvey Cashore and Frédéric Zalac, "Names of SNC employees, executives behind thousands of dollars in illegal Liberal Party donations revealed," The Fifth Estate, CBC, April 30, 2019, *https://www.cbc.ca/news/politics/snc-lavalin-liberal-donors-list-canada-elections-1.5114537.*

170   Dion, *Trudeau II.*

in the upcoming budget. A Criminal Code amendment, in the budget. A bill about spending, but with a special section added in there, buried deep in the back, custom-designed for SNC-Lavalin so it could slither out of criminal corruption charges with a lame apology and a promise never to do it again.

And again, the most incredible part: *That's exactly what the Liberals did!*

This was the 2018 budget that weighed in at an incredible 582 pages. The massive omnibus bill that the Liberals had promised they would never, ever use, unlike that mean old Stephen Harper. And deep in the depths of this gargantuan omnibus bill, the SNC-Lavalin Slap-on-the-Wrist Criminal Code Amendment, as it might as well be called, was buried on page 527. This was the secret clause that was so well hidden that even government MPs didn't know it was there. This was the one that Liberal MP Greg Fergus told the House of Commons finance committee that he had missed completely in his review of the budget, and later said he had "serious questions" about it; that "It seems we're letting those with the means have an easier time of it than those who don't have the means."[171]

As Dion, the ethics commissioner, noted in his *Trudeau II* report, "Several witnesses interviewed were of the view that non-fiscal items are typically included in a federal budget bill to expedite passage through Parliament."[172] In other words, it was hidden so it could be slipped past Parliament more easily, without proper examination or debate. That's what SNC-Lavalin wanted, and that's exactly what the Liberals delivered.

But that wasn't enough for SNC-Lavalin — or for their Librano friends. The bill that would implement the budget, Bill C-74, received Royal Assent on June 21, 2018, less than six months after Bruce had arranged to run into Bill Morneau at the World Economic Forum in Switzerland. You have to hand it to Bruce: He got results, fast. Head-

---

171   Andy Blatchford, "Federal budget bill quietly proposes tool to ease penalties for corporate crime," CBC News, May 15, 2018, *https://www.cbc.ca/news/politics/federal-budget-corporate-wrongdoing-1.4664490.*

172   Dion, *Trudeau II.*

spinningly fast. So it's little wonder that he felt that he could always ask for more. After all, the Liberals had been so quick and efficient in doing the company's bidding up until now. They had followed SNC-Lavalin's directions to the letter. They were even more compliant than the Gadhafis were.

So, by August 2018, just two months later, SNC-Lavalin decided to complain to Ben Chin, then the chief of staff to Finance Minister Morneau, that it had been weeks since the budget bill had passed, and yet here they were still facing charges. What on earth was taking so long? This wasn't the kind of service they had come to expect from this government. As Dion noted in his report, recounting a conversation between Chin and Jessica Prince, the chief of staff to the then attorney general and minister of justice, Jody Wilson-Raybould: "Mr. Chin stated that he had been speaking with SNC-Lavalin, and that the company's perception was that the process of negotiating a remediation agreement was taking too long. Mr. Chin asked whether anything could be done to expedite the process."[173]

This was the first moment where the SNC-Lavalin/Libranos corporate-government partnership started to really step in its own excrement. The very idea of a government minister trying to get a peek inside the independent office of the Public Prosecution Service of Canada was a major problem. This was supposed to be a justice system, not an arm of Bill Morneau's corporate-favouritism department, or a branch office of Justin Trudeau's Librano family compact. As Dion notes: "Ms. Prince informed Mr. Chin that a senior official with the Public Prosecution Service of Canada (Prosecution Service) had previously informed staff within the office of the Minister of Justice and Attorney General that they could not seek an update from the Prosecution Service. Ms. Prince wrote that since the Prosecution Service is statutorily independent of government, simply asking for a status update could be perceived as, and may be, improper political interference."[174]

---

173   ibid.

174   ibid.

Now, it's worth noting that this was sort of a new situation that the Liberals found themselves in — and it was designed exactly to catch them in the kind of scandals they had become notorious for over the last decades. In fact, the very reason that the Public Prosecution Service of Canada existed was as a response to the Libranos' last unholy scandal, the sponsorship scandal, or Adscam.

In 2006, the Conservative government under Stephen Harper was elected after voters grew disgusted with the Liberals and revelations of their scheme to funnel money to Liberal-friendly cronies using a program designed to fund pro-federalist advertising in Quebec — Adscam. The trouble was that, while some of Liberal cronies connected to the ad agencies that took the illegal cash were prosecuted, no senior Liberal politicians ever were. As a story by Janice Tibbetts with the CanWest News Service (now Postmedia) explained at the time: "Fraud charges — such as those laid in the federal sponsorship scandal — are currently prosecuted provincially because provincial governments are responsible for administering the Criminal Code." The Harper government wanted to set up an independent federal office to prosecute federal crimes — and one that could not be meddled with.[175] As Tibbetts explained: "Under the current system, police investigate crimes and lay charges, but often consult with federal and provincial Crowns on how to proceed, leaving the process vulnerable to interference from political bosses."

So it was the Libranos themselves who had inspired the Director of Public Prosecutions Act. It was like a tripwire to catch their meddling in the judicial process. As Conservative MP Pierre Poilievre told the committee studying the bill in 2006: "The reason (the Director of Public Prosecutions Act) was proposed in the last election — and I'm not afraid to say it — is that a lot of people were confused about the fact that a number of advertising agencies were pursued with legal action when one organization, which was clearly at the centre of the same

---

175   Janice Tibbetts, "Harper aims to limit political control of judicial system," *Edmonton Journal*, April 12, 2006.

scandal and benefited directly from it without any question whatsoever … was not."[176] That organization? The Liberal Party of Canada.

No wonder the Liberals didn't like the independent prosecution service. Gerald Butts, the prime minister's best friend, top aide and strategic brains had even allegedly said they should just ignore it, when he was explaining to Wilson-Raybould why the government needed to interfere to put a stop to the prosecution of SNC-Lavalin. Butts had told Wilson-Raybould's staff, according to what her own record of these discussions alleged, that "there is no solution here that doesn't involve some interference."[177] According to Wilson-Raybould, Butts allegedly told her— the attorney general — that this Director of Public Prosecutions Act was law that "was set up by Harper" and "he does not like the law."[178]

Add it to the list of laws that the Liberals didn't think applied to them. Like the one that says prime ministers shouldn't solicit and accept gifts from billionaires who are in the middle of doing business with the federal government. Or like the one that says that lucrative fishing licences that are ultimately owned by the public shouldn't be handed out to their relatives just so they can get rich from them. You really have to wonder: Are there any laws that the Liberals think they should have to follow? Or are they so sure of their own superiority compared to everyone else, that they literally think they are above the law? Actually, you don't have to wonder. It's blatantly obvious they think they're above the law. That's how the Libranos roll.

---

176   Evidence of meeting #18 for Bill C-2 (39th Parliament, 1st Session) in the 39th Parliament, 1st Session, *https://openparliament.ca/committees/bill-c-2-39-1/39-1/18/pierre-poilievre-2/*.

177   "Read Jody Wilson-Raybould's opening statement on the SNC-Lavalin affair," CBC News, Feb. 27, 2019, *https://www.cbc.ca/news/politics/jody-wilson-raybould-opening-statements-1.5035785*.

178   Tristin Hopper, "The Harper government passed a measure 13 years ago to catch Liberal scandals. It worked perfectly," *National Post*, March 1, 2019, *https://nationalpost.com/news/politics/the-tories-passed-a-measure-designed-to-catch-liberal-scandals-thirteen-years-later-it-caught-lavscam*.

Well, Butts and his fellow Libranos were about to "not like" the DPP Act a lot more, very shortly. It wasn't long after the finance minister's minions had tried meddling in the prosecutor's office's independent investigation into SNC-Lavalin because the company had told the Liberals it "was taking too long" to get them a settlement. That was in August 2018; by September, the prosecutors finally had some long-awaited news for the company. Only, it wasn't the news the company — or their flunkies in the Liberal government — were expecting. The independent prosecutors' office had decided that a deferred-prosecution agreement, or remediation agreement, was "inappropriate" for SNC-Lavalin. The company would continue to be prosecuted for corruption and bribery.[179]

Just imagine the shock and the horror that reverberated through SNC-Lavalin, this company that had always been able to grease its way through the corridors of government power from Gadhafi's Libya to Trudeau's Libranos. After having custom designed its own punishment, and managing to get the Liberals to sneak it past Parliament in the back of a monstrous omnibus budget bill. Just imagine the outrage in the backrooms of the Liberal government as Bill Morneau, Justin Trudeau, Gerald Butts, and everyone else who had been working overtime to execute the company's underhanded schemes — who had written a law specifically to let their buddies get away without answering for corruption charges — had seen all their work undone by an independent public prosecutor. The very independent prosecutor office set up by the Harper Conservatives to do this very thing had perfectly foiled the Liberals. Imagine their fury that they had been stopped from corrupting the Canadian justice system to help out their dirty friends. Imagine all the eyes popping. The faces bulging red. The teeth gnashing.

It's kind of fun to think about it, isn't it?

---

179   Dion, *Trudeau II.*

CHAPTER 8

THE FAKE FEMINIST
LASHES OUT

It was scarcely four years ago when Justin Trudeau uttered three words that would make him seem to credulous women around the world that he was a superstar feminist. You know the three words. Everyone knows the three words. They were heard around the world. They were a brilliant political masterstroke. Even if they were hiding a darker truth. Maybe that's what made them so brilliant: That they let Trudeau get away for so long with acting like the exact opposite of what those three words convinced people he stood for.

After being sworn in as prime minister Trudeau revealed his cabinet made up of equal numbers of men and women, appointed based on which sex they belonged to, not their qualifications. That's a pretty big risk with a rookie team; there weren't a lot of qualified candidates eager to run for a party that had been in third place when the 2015 election was called, and stayed in third place in the polls for a long stretch through the election itself, until its fortunes suddenly turned toward the end of the race. "Some people who got in were borderline idiots," one Liberal insider told the *National Post*'s John Ivison.[180] You might even have an idea who those idiots are. Meanwhile more than half-a-dozen of those first-day cabinet ministers — from Hunter Tootoo, to Seamus O'Regan, to Maryam Monsef, to Harjit Sajjan, to Bill Morneau, to Dominic LeBlanc, to Kent Hehr — would in the coming years be embroiled in one scandal or another, ranging from substance abuse (Tootoo and O'Regan) to sexual misconduct allegations (Hehr and allegedly Tootoo), to accepting political favours (O'Regan again), to patronage (Leblanc), to misrepresenting their past (Morneau, Monsef and Sajjan, who was caught lying about his military career — he publicly claimed he was the "architect" of an Afghan military operation, but actually wasn't).[181] Literally 20 per cent of Trudeau's cabinet-by-gender would end up caught up in some scandal or other in their very first term. Maybe counting genitals isn't such a great way to pick a cabinet after all.

Meanwhile, Trudeau's new cabinet-making process sidelined a good number of smart, qualified men who didn't fit with his desire for cosmetic diversity: retired lieutenant general Andrew Leslie (who has announced he won't be running for the Liberals again in 2019), former Indian Affairs minister Bob Nault and former solicitor general Wayne Easter. "There's a bias in this government against anyone older than 40," one veteran told Ivison.[182] Which is weird, when you consider that when Trudeau was elected, he was nearly 45.

But Trudeau thought the kids' birthday-party-seating-plan strategy of boy-girl/boy-girl was just the coolest idea ever for building the cabinet of a G7 nation. And he was eager and ready to brag about what a no-brainer it was when some reporter threw him the question he had been waiting for: Say, Mr. Prime Minister, why did you appoint an equal number of men and women?

---

180   John Ivison, *Trudeau: The Education of a Prime Minister* (Toronto; Signal), 2019. p. 126-7.

181   Kathleen Harris, "'Stolen valour': Sajjan faces calls to resign in wake of Afghanistan battle claim," CBC News, May 1, 2017, *https://www.cbc.ca/news/politics/sajjan-apology-operation-medusa-1.4093270.*

182   ibid.

"Because it's 2015."

It was a line made to go viral. The crowd assembled that day at Rideau Hall cheered. Headline writers around the world lapped it up. Celebrities, including British actress Emma Watson, tweeted their enthusiastic approval. So did the United Nation's office for women.[183]

What had come across like an off-the-cuff, duh-isn't-it-obvious? remark, had been under development for years as a Liberal zinger, Trudeau's best friend and top strategist, Gerald Butts, would later reveal.[184] But that just reveals how brilliant — and cynical — the whole ploy was. Trudeau earned with those three words a massive bank of capital as a world-leading feminist. (Never mind that the swearing in of those same female cabinet ministers that same day featured Trudeau grabbing both their arms, pulling his face up to their noses and grinning as he subjected them to an uncomfortably long stare that bored through their eyes and into the back of their skulls.)

After those three words, and the gush of joy that followed it from women and gender-progressives around the world, it would take a lot for anyone to question his gender-equality bona fides.

Yet, within barely more than three years, Trudeau would provide more than enough proof to Canada and the world that he was anything but a feminist. That the entire act was a calculated fraud by a man with a history of allegations that he molested young women, and who even today, cannot tolerate any powerful woman who challenges his dominance. Women including two of those who were sworn into cabinet that warm November day at Rideau Hall, Jody Wilson-Raybould and Jane Philpott. Trudeau had seen them as mere props in his virtue-signalling image management. It turns out, much to his annoyance, that they had minds of their own. And Trudeau would make them pay for that.

---

183   Adam Frisk, "'Because it's 2015': Trudeau's gender-equal cabinet makes headlines around world, social media," Global News, Nov. 5, 2015, *https://globalnews. ca/news/2320795/because-its-2015-trudeaus-gender-equal-cabinet-makes-headlines-around-world-social-media/.*

184   Ivison, *Trudeau.*

It's interesting that both those women were well over 40, even older than Trudeau, and highly accomplished in their careers before joining his team. Hey, maybe that's why he prefers his cabinet women young — maybe he thinks it makes them easier to control.

As much feminist capital as Trudeau had built up with his concocted, tailored-for-Twitter cabinet performance, it didn't take long for the mask to slip just a little. Just a few months later, in the House of Commons, Trudeau lost his temper and physically assaulted a young, female member of the NDP, Ruth Ellen Brosseau, aged 32 years old at the time.[185]

To repeat: Trudeau. Hit. A. Woman. On the floor of the House of Commons. Just months after he had been praised as a world-leading feminist prime minister. Trudeau insisted it was an accident and apologized.[186] He kind of had to: The Speaker of the House had criticized him for it: "It is not appropriate to manhandle other members," Speaker Geoff Regan castigated Trudeau.[187] But why did he do it? Because, according to accounts from those who witnessed it that day, he had lost his temper. The MPs were coming in for a vote on a government bill, and he thought they were taking too long to get to their seats. So the prime minister stormed onto the floor to grab the Conservative party whip, Gordon Brown, and physically drag him to his seat.[188]

"He looked very, very angry and he pushed some people, grabbed the arm of the whip and pulled him saying stuff like, you know, 'get the f–k out of my way,' and when he turned back he hit Ruth Ellen Brosseau and she was shocked and hurt. So he pulled [Brown] to the end of the

---

185   "An oral history of Elbowgate," *Maclean's*, May 21, 2016, *https://www. macleans.ca/politics/ottawa/an-oral-history-of-elbowgate/*.

186   Andrew Russell, "Trudeau apologizes again in House of Commons for elbowing incident," Global News, May 19, 2016, *https://globalnews.ca/news/2710867/ trudeau-apologizes-again-in-house-of-commons-for-elbowing-incident/*.

187   Emma Loop, "House Of Commons Erupts After Justin Trudeau Elbows An Opposition MP," Buzzfeed News, May 18, 2016, *https://www.buzzfeed.com/ emmaloop/justin-trudeau-got-physical-with-an-opposition-mp-and-had-to*.

188   "An oral," *Maclean's*.

room," recounted one NDP MP. Another added: "He said, 'Get the bleep out of the way.' There was some resistance by the whip [Brown] and on the final pull he elbowed Ruth Ellen Brosseau and knocked her over. Ruth Ellen was clutching her breast and her chest and she had a big red mark on her chest."

Huh. So Justin Trudeau, woke progressive feminist, barked "get the f—k out of my way" to the young female elected MP, before driving his elbow into her breast. Because he wanted to violently take control of a situation. Huh.

That wasn't going to be the end of Brosseau's victimization at the hands of Liberals: While the injury was "very painful," she later told the Canadian Press, she was then harassed by Trudeau fans who tried to tell her it was all her fault. "My office has received countless phone calls ... saying it is my fault, I should be ashamed, I should resign, I should apologize, it is my fault," she said, looking "visibly shaken," according to the report. "And then (people are asking), 'Was she hit hard enough in the breast?' Do I have justify how hard I was hit in the breast? It doesn't matter."[189]

Huh. So a young woman is assaulted by a male prime minister, and Liberals tell her it's her fault. That she was asking for it. Because, um … it was 2016?

It would soon turn out that this wasn't the first time the arch-feminist Trudeau had been unpleasantly physical with a young woman.

Trudeau acted as if none of this was happening. He continued to fake his feminism all over the world. In 2017, he attended the Annual Women in the World Summit in New York City. "This is part of a habit — a good habit — I've developed, wherever I go, to sit down with extraordinary leaders, particularly in business, who happen to be

---

189   Kristy Kirkup, "Ruth Ellen Brosseau target of personal attacks since being elbowed by Trudeau," *Maclean's*, May 20, 2016, *https://www.cbc.ca/news/politics/ brosseau-trudeau-elbowing-attacks-1.3590066.*

women and talk about what more we can do," Trudeau congratulated himself at a morning roundtable with female business leaders.[190]

A few weeks later, he announced he would spend $20 million of federal money on a group called Women Deliver. "Everyone benefits from a more gender equal world, but little progress on gender equality can be made without a strong focus on the health and wellbeing of women and girls, especially their sexual and reproductive health and rights," he said at the time.[191] Later that same year, he announced his government was changing a government-grant program to fund summer jobs at places like children's camps and day cares: Any group that didn't sign an attestation that it would not oppose abortion could no longer qualify for the grant.[192] That would immediately disqualify Christian, Muslim and other faith-based organizations. Extreme abortion-rights feminists celebrated.[193] Everyone else — even erstwhile liberals — shuddered at the ideological authoritarianism.[194]

Trudeau was working hard to rebuild his feminist cred after the scandal of having violently assaulted a young woman in a rage. And he didn't care how much of the public's money he had to spend, or steer in rigid ideological directions, in order to do it. But no matter how hard he tried, all the spending announcements, conference-hopping and abortion extremism couldn't keep up with the growing scandals

190   "Justin Trudeau In New York City To Attend Annual Women In The World Summit," *Huffington Post*, April 6, 2017, *https://www.huffingtonpost.ca/2017/04/06/trudeau-new-york-women-summit_n_15848258.html*.

191   Kenneth Chan, "Trudeau announces Vancouver as host city of Women Deliver Conference in 2019," *Daily Hive*, June 13, 2017, *https://dailyhive.com/vancouver/vancouver-women-deliver-conference-2019*.

192   Amanda Connolly, "Government looking to shut down summer job grants for anti-abortion groups," *iPolitics*, April 13, 2017, *https://ipolitics.ca/2017/04/13/government-shutting-down-summer-job-grants-for-anti-abortion-groups-source/*.

193   Joyce Arthur, "Canada Summer Jobs kerfuffle: Full of sound and fury, signifying nothing," *rabble.ca*, Feb. 2, 2018, *http://rabble.ca/columnists/2018/02/canada-summer-jobs-kerfuffle-full-sound-and-fury-signifying-nothing*.

194   Lorna Dueck, "Faith-based students should never be denied a summer job," *The Globe and Mail*, March 21, 2018, *https://www.theglobeandmail.com/inside-the-globe/article-how-to-apply-for-the-globe-and-mails-2019-summer-job-program/*.

around the disrespectful and dominating way he was actually treating women in real life.

In January 2018, a woman went public with allegations that one of Trudeau's cabinet ministers, Kent Hehr, had been sexually aggressive with her and other women back when he was an MLA in Alberta. "My first day working at the Alberta legislature I was told to avoid being in [an] elevator with Kent Hehr. He would make comments. He would make you feel unsafe," revealed Kristin Raworth, now an advocate for survivors of sexual violence, on Twitter, to add her voice to the #MeToo movement that was then becoming a global force. "There is literally no woman who worked in the annex who didn't experience this. He made verbally sexually suggestive comments to all of us," Raworth went on. "In an elevator with me and only me said 'you're yummy'." He was known, she said, as "the man who scares you in an elevator." She then said that six other women had come forward to her the night she tweeted that story, with similar allegations. "I imagine this is the tip of the iceberg." And she challenged Trudeau to "get rid of him."[195]

Spoiler alert: Trudeau ignored the women and stood by Hehr, an alleged predator of young women in elevators. Hehr is still in Trudeau's supposedly ultra-feminist Liberal caucus.[196] He'll be running for the Liberals again in 2019 in Calgary. Trudeau has since shown up to throw his support behind Hehr in public appearances. "He's a strong member of the team," he said visiting Hehr's riding Stampede breakfast just months after Raworth had levelled her serious and credible allegations of sexual misconduct against Hehr. "We're so lucky to have him," Trudeau said. He called Hehr a "great MP."[197]

---

195   Kristin Raworth on Twitter (@KristinRaworth), Jan. 24, 2018.

196   Peter Zimonjic, "Hehr won't return to cabinet, but remains in Liberal caucus after harassment investigation," CBC News, June 6, 2018, *https://www.cbc.ca/news/politics/hehr-harassment-report-liberal-1.4694165.*

197   James Wood, "Trudeau backs Hehr as tough political battle looms," *Calgary Herald,* July 7, 2018, *https://calgaryherald.com/news/politics/hes-a-strong-member-of-the-team-trudeau-backs-hehr-as-tough-political-battle-looms.*

In reality, Trudeau was in a jam, tied up in a web of fake-feminist lies of his own. Just weeks before he showed up in Calgary to praise elevator operator Kent Hehr, Trudeau had found himself exposed, too. In June 2018, former Liberal strategist Warren Kinsella published on his blog an editorial that had appeared 18 years earlier in the *Creston Valley Advance* newspaper. It was written by a young reporter, who would later come forward as one Rose Knight, who was also reporting that day for the *National Post*.[198] She was alleging that Trudeau had groped her while he was in Creston for the Kokanee Summit, a beer festival that in 2018, its second year, was also raising money for the Kokanee Glacier Alpine Campaign. That was a campaign launched by the Trudeau family to raise money for a backcountry cabin in memory of Justin's brother Michel, who was killed in a B.C. avalanche in 1998 while backcountry skiing.[199] Trudeau was at the drunken beer fest that year to celebrate the cause.

Knight's August 2000 article began by quoting the lame apology she alleged Trudeau had given her after he had gotten physical with her — without her consent: "I'm sorry. If I had known you were reporting for a national paper, I never would have been so forward." Knight went on: "Trudeau, who was in Creston to celebrate the Kokanee Summit festival put on by the Columbia Brewery, apologized — a day late — for inappropriately 'handling' the reporter while she was on assignment not only for the *Advance* but also for the *National Post* and *Vancouver Sun*."[200]

Knight, just 28 at the time, sadly acknowledged that it wasn't exactly "rare" for "a young reporter, especially a female who is working for a small community newspaper [to] be considered an underling to their 'more predominant' associates and blatantly disrespected because of it.

---

198   Douglas Quan, Adrian Humphreys and Marie-Danielle Smith, "Why an 18-year-old groping allegation against Justin Trudeau is not a #MeToo moment," *National Post*, June 22, 2018, *https://nationalpost.com/news/politics/why-an-18-year-old-groping-allegation-against-justin-trudeau-is-not-a-metoo-moment*.

199   Wikipedia, "Michel Trudeau," *https://en.wikipedia.org/wiki/Michel_Trudeau*.

200   Quan, Humphreys and Smith, "Why."

"But shouldn't the son of a former prime minister be aware of the rights and wrongs that go along with public socializing? Didn't he learn, through his vast experiences in public life, that groping a strange young woman isn't in the handbook of proper etiquette, regardless of who she is, what her business is or where they are?

"And what makes the fact that she was working for the *Post* of any relevance?"[201]

Valerie Bourne who was publisher of the *Advance* at the time, later told the National Post that Knight had told her about the "inappropriate handling" and remembers that Knight "was distressed." The editor at the time, Brian Bell, who was away on the day it happened, heard from Knight, too. "I believe that it happened," Bell later said. "I know that she told me about it when I got back and I don't doubt she spoke to the publisher about it."[202]

And what was Trudeau's response to this stunning allegation of sexual assault? What did the Liberal leader have to say, who in 2014 said we must "give the benefit of the doubt to those who come forward" with allegations?[203] The prime minister who bragged that had a zero-tolerance policy for sexual misconduct and had even once fired two MPs on the mere accusation of a serial complainant who was member of a rival party?[204] The uber-feminist Trudeau who had self-righteously told CBC News just a few months prior that "There is no context in which someone doesn't have responsibility for things they've done in the past"? Who assured the CBC that he was the most respectful man ever, saying "I've been very, very careful all my life to be thoughtful, to be respectful of people's space and people's headspace as well"? Who

---

201   ibid.

202   ibid.

203   Jason Fekete et al., "Trudeau suspends two Liberal MPs from caucus for alleged 'personal misconduct," *Ottawa Citizen*, Nov. 6, 2014, *https://ottawacitizen. com/news/politics/two-liberal-mps-investigated-for-personal-misconduct.*

204   Christie Blatchford, "Christine Moore may not be the feminist conscience she branded herself to be," *National Post*, May 8, 2018, *https://nationalpost.com/ opinion/christie-blatchford-moore-may-not-be-the-feminist-conscience-she-has-branded-herself-to-be.*

vowed that even he, the prime minister, should be held to account, just like any man, for how he treats women?[205]

He waved the whole thing off.

He said he didn't recall any "negative interactions" that day.[206]

Just like the women who were brave enough to come forward about their fear of Kent Hehr, he hung yet another alleged victim of sexual assault out to dry.

And his supporters said her story didn't "matter" because it had happened 18 years before. They denied Rose Knight her own truth.[207]

Finally, so did Trudeau. Weeks after the scandal had kept sizzling, refusing to just go away, he simply went ahead and dismissed Knight's account as false. "I am confident that I did not act inappropriately," he said. "I'll be blunt about it — often a man experiences an interaction as being benign or not inappropriate, and a woman, particularly in a professional context, can experience it differently."[208]

Of course. You know how those women can be. So hyper-sensitive to what their male counterparts properly understand to be "benign or not inappropriate." Obviously you'd have to be hysterical to think that Justin Trudeau, of all people, could have possibly done anything inappropriate, let alone gropey.

Except… then why did he apologize? Why did he say he wouldn't have done it if he had known she was reporting for a national newspaper?

---

205   Catharine Tunney, "Trudeau says zero tolerance on misconduct toward women applies to him as well," CBC News, Jan 30, 2018, *https://www.cbc.ca/news/politics/trudeau-careful-metoo-1.4511093.*

206   Quan, Humphreys and Smith, "Why."

207   Anne Kingston, "Why Justin Trudeau's reported 'Kokanee Grope' really matters," *Maclean's*, June 27, 2018, *https://www.macleans.ca/news/canada/justin-trudeaus-reported-kokanee-grope-matters-but-not-for-the-obvious-reason/.*

208   Brian Lilley, "Liberals' sexual harassment training mandated by Kokanee grope PM hypocritical," *Toronto Sun*, Jan. 10, 2019, *https://torontosun.com/opinion/columnists/lilley-liberals-sexual-harassment-training-mandated-by-kokanee-grope-pm-hypocritical.*

Or was Rose Knight, this supposedly oversensitive, hysterical young woman, imagining all of that, too?

Whatever lame excuses Trudeau had offered for his behaviour that day, the mask had now slipped completely. The Liberals began to lose popularity in the polls. They showed even former Liberal supporters were starting to feel repulsed out by the fraudulent, fondling feminist.[209]

And a few months later, a woman from Trudeau's own caucus, went public with claims that he had no time for the opinions and ideas of females like her. Leona Alleslev, a former captain in the Royal Canadian Air Force who, as an impressive Liberal candidate, had taken the Aurora—Oak Ridges—Richmond Hill away from the Tory incumbent in 2015. She was over 40 years old at the time. She said she had tried to raise with the prime minister about military and economic issues. "My attempts to raise my concerns with this government were met with silence," Alleslev said.[210] She declared she was crossing the floor to the Conservatives.

Here was another strong woman who dared to try challenging Trudeau. And here was another strong woman who found that Trudeau wouldn't stand for it.

And she certainly wouldn't be the last.

---

209   "Kokanee Grope gives poll numbers a nudge," *Toronto Sun*, July 22, 2018, *https://torontosun.com/opinion/editorials/editorial-kokanee-grope-gives-poll-numbers-a-nudge*.

210   "MP Leona Alleslev on why she crossed the floor from the Liberals to the Tories," *Maclean's*, Sept. 17, 2018, *https://www.macleans.ca/politics/ottawa/mp-leona-alleslev-on-why-she-crossed-the-floor-from-the-liberals-to-the-tories/*.

CHAPTER 9

TRUDEAU DECIDES TO DESTROY JODY WILSON-RAYBOULD

After Justin Trudeau's miserable summer of 2018, it finally started to look as if the waves of accusations, allegations and galling hypocrisies that had for months been relentlessly eroding his credibility as a progressive feminist had finally stopped. Now, with an election coming just about a year away, he desperately needed to start patching up the cracks in his phony image.

So, naturally, he reverted to the old formula. In September, he turned up at the Women in the World Canada conference in Toronto, where he dusted off his old script about the importance of helping women advance in their careers. [211] He even talked with a straight face about preventing sexual harassment, which can limit their advancement. He didn't mention his own run-in with Rose Knight, who was just

---

211   "Fighting sexual harassment helps women rise through ranks: Trudeau," CBC News, Sept. 10, 2018, *https://www.cbc.ca/news/politics/trudeau-toronto-women-summit-1.4816846.*

trying to do her job when he groped her, and had since quit her own journalism career. That would be the same conference where Foreign Minister Chrystia Freeland appeared on an extremist anti-Donald-Trump panel, called "Taking on the Tyrant" — right in the midst of her flailing attempts to salvage NAFTA as Trump was threatening to tear up Canada's most important free-trade deal, and with it devastate much of Canada's economy. As if the democratically elected president of the United States, our closest ally and most important trading partner, were on par with Syria's Bashar al-Assad.[212]

Then in August, his government, through the traditional diplomatic channel of Freeland's Twitter account, stuck a finger in the eye of the Saudi regime by tweeting about the Arab kingdom's treatment of women's-rights activists. "Canada is gravely concerned about additional arrests of civil society and women's rights activists in Saudi Arabia, including Samar Badawi. We urge the Saudi authorities to immediately release them and all other peaceful human rights activists," Freeland tweeted. She may have been right, but it was a showy, pointless gesture that accomplished nothing except to perhaps help burnish her boss's faltering feminist image. The Saudis simply slapped sanctions on Canada in response.[213] It's true the Saudis are absolutely notorious abusers of human rights, but the Liberal government had never felt strongly enough about it before then to actually cancel the sale of Canadian weapons that were ostensibly being used to oppress the kingdom's subjects.[214] Freeland's tweet, like Trudeau's entire feminist posture, was all show, no action; all image, no substance.

But never mind the cost of sanctions for no actual achievable point whatsoever: Trudeau had a badly tattered illusion to repair.

---

212   John Ivison, "Liberals eye potential electoral gains from 'taking on the tyrant' Trump," *National Post*, Sept. 12, 2018, *https://nationalpost.com/opinion/john-ivison-liberals-eye-potential-electoral-gains-from-taking-on-the-tyrant-trump*.

213   "Freeland defends Canada's stance on Saudi Arabia amid sanctions," CBC News, Aug. 6, 2018, *https://www.cbc.ca/news/politics/canada-saudi-diplomacy-reaction-1.4775545*.

214   Janyce McGregor, "'Difficult contract' binds Canada to Saudi LAV deal, Trudeau says," CBC News, Oct. 23, 2018, *https://www.cbc.ca/news/politics/trudeau-metro-morning-lavs-saudis-1.4874383*.

And that meant, as usual, hauling out the most extreme tool he could find from his now-familiar toolkit: The pandering to the most extreme feminists; the women's-studies professors and the male-haters. It would be from the same mould as his decision to ban faith groups who refused to support abortion from a grant to hire camp counsellors and other summer students. Trudeau decided to publicly accuse all male manual labourers of being rapists. Trudeau was at the G20 Summit in Argentina in late 2018, participating in a panel on "gender-equality." (Naturally. Have you noticed the seeming lack of invitations for our prime minister to sit on panels about improving the business investment climate?)

He was explaining to his audience why his new rules for approving pipelines and other major infrastructure projects would include all kinds of non-scientific criteria that had nothing to do with economic or environmental impacts. Among the woolier considerations, in addition to "traditional knowledge" of local Aboriginals, there was the worst one of all: "gender impacts." For months Canadians had been scratching their heads at how a pipeline or an electricity corridor might have any impact on gender issues. Well, Trudeau was finally ready with an explanation, and it was utterly unhinged:

"You might say, 'What does a gender lens have to do with building this new highway or this new pipeline?'" he said. "Well, there are impacts when you bring construction workers into a rural area — there are social impacts because they are mostly male construction workers. How are you adjusting or adapting to those [impacts]?"[215] In other words, all those men in a rural area would bring nothing but trouble to the poor, helpless country lasses. You know, drunken brawls, urinating on the cow sheds, and, of course, rape.

Now, to be fair, Trudeau has probably only met the handful of construction workers that have traipsed in and out of his family's various palatial homes while he redoes the kitchen or installs a new wine cellar. Or maybe he avoided them entirely, for fear of the gender

---

215   "Trudeau unacceptably smears construction workers," *Toronto Sun*, Dec. 3, 2018, *https://torontosun.com/opinion/editorials/editorial-trudeau-unacceptably-smears-construction-workers.*

impacts he might feel. But women who actually know construction workers in real life were outraged. "Personally when I saw this video it made my blood boil as my husband oversees a crew in the natural gas division. He sacrifices for our family by being out of town for work," wrote Tamara Mack Robbins on Facebook. "These are not 'frat boys' the workers he refers to are our husbands, sons, brothers and, yes, sisters. How dare he speak this way of my husband and many Canadian families!"[216] Male workers themselves and the energy and construction industry groups[217, 218] spoke out loudly against the outrageous smear.

But the extreme and inflammatory comment had exactly the effect that Trudeau wanted. It earned back some of his squandered feminist credibility with the most extreme voices on the anti-male left.[219, 220] And if he could keep them onside, then he would be more immune to accusations about his own chauvinist behaviour.

But then another one of those uppity female MPs had to go and start thinking for themselves and make trouble for poor Justin all over again.

The next to step up and call Trudeau a fraud? Celina Caesar-Chavannes, formerly a vice-chair of the governing council of the University of Toronto's Scarborough campus, and a former Toronto Board of Trade

---

216   ibid.

217   Katie Dangerfield, "Oil worker confronts Trudeau on his 'gender impact' comment — but he dodges question," Global News, Jan. 11, 2019, *https://globalnews.ca/news/4837456/justin-trudeau-gender-impact-construction-workers/*.

218   Angela Gismondi, "Industry slams Trudeau on 'gender impacts' comment about male construction workers," *Daily Commercial News*, Dec. 6, 2018, *https://canada.constructconnect.com/dcn/news/government/2018/12/industry-slams-trudeau-gender-impacts-comment-male-construction-workers*.

219   Kevin Maimann, "Link between rural work camps and violence against women is real, researchers say," *StarMetro Edmonton*, Dec. 4, 2018, *https://www.thestar.com/edmonton/2018/12/04/link-between-rural-work-camps-and-violence-against-women-is-real-researchers-say.html*.

220   "Man Camps" thread, *rabble.ca* discussion forums, *http://www.rabble.ca/babble/labour-and-consumption/man-camps*.

Business Entrepreneur of the Year.[221] She was accomplished and — yes — over 40. Trudeau should have known she might have some of those pesky opinions and ideas of her own.

And worst of all for Trudeau's woke, progressive reputation: Caesar-Chavannes is a woman of colour — black and proud of it.

So in March 2019, she had the temerity to inform Trudeau that she was done with the party, after one term, and would not be running again for him in her riding of Whitby. His reaction, she says, was another one of those burst of rages, which sounded much like the one he showed to Ruth Ellen Brosseau as he assaulted her on the floor of the House of Commons. "He was yelling," said Caesar-Chavannes. "He was yelling that I didn't appreciate him, that he'd given me so much." She posted on her personal Twitter account a quote from the prime minister: "I believe real leadership is about listening, learning & compassion...central to my leadership is fostering an environment where my Ministers, caucus & staff feel comfortable coming to me when they have concerns."

Then she added her own comment: "I did come to you recently. Twice. Remember your reactions?"[222]

As usual the Prime Minister's Office called her a liar; it said that Trudeau had displayed "absolutely no hostility."[223] Obviously she's just another one of those oversensitive broads who insists on experiencing things differently.

She, too, wouldn't be the last.

Because while Caesar-Chavannes was allegedly listening to her feminist male boss rant about how she didn't appreciate how much he had

---

221   Wikipedia, "Celina Caesar-Chavannes," *https://en.wikipedia.org/wiki/Celina_Caesar-Chavannes*.

222   Celina Caesar-Chavannes Twitter account (@MPCelina), March 7, 2019, *https://twitter.com/MPCelina/status/1103680760337260545*.

223   Kathleen Harris, "MP Celina Caesar-Chavannes quits Liberal caucus," CBC News, March 20, 2019, *https://www.cbc.ca/news/politics/liberal-mp-caesar-chavannes-caucus-1.5064544*.

"given" her — because, you know, there's no way she could have actually earned her success herself — a bigger mushroom cloud was spreading over Brand Trudeau. And it was detonated by yet another of those troublesome Liberal women of colour.

It was the revenge of Jody Wilson-Raybould.

When in September 2018 the fully independent Director of Public Prosecutions office informed Wilson-Raybould, then the attorney general and justice minister, that it had concluded that a deferred-prosecution/remediation agreement was not appropriate for SNC-Lavalin, Wilson-Raybould knew there would be blowback from her bosses.

The law still did allow her to overrule the DPP, but to do so legally under the law set up by Harper's Conservatives, she would have to announce that she was doing so publicly. There could be no secret overruling, leaving the public in the dark. The minister would have to be publicly accountable for making such a decision. And so, as she would later tell the ethics commissioner, "she sought to be entirely confident in her decision not to take any action."[224] She had her chief of staff, Jessica Prince, engage in discussions throughout the ministry and department in order to sound out the decision. Wilson-Raybould herself directly solicited advice from "several" former attorneys general. She read through the documentation.

She did her homework. She exercised her judgment. She was sure of her decision.

She was obviously going to be trouble for a prime minister who preferred his female ministers to be compliant props.

So, when Trudeau had a meeting scheduled with Wilson-Raybould in mid-September, "to discuss a topic unrelated to SNC-Lavalin," he couldn't resist lecturing her about that exact topic and her office's

---

224   Mario Dion, *Trudeau II Report made under the Conflict of Interest Act*, Office of the Conflict of Interest and Ethics Commissioner, August 2019, *http:// ciec-ccie.parl.gc.ca/Documents/English/Public%20Reports/Examination%20Reports/ Trudeau%20II%20Report.pdf.*

decision not to interfere in the prosecution. According to Wilson-Raybould's notes, he warned her "the company would move from Montreal," where he represented the Papineau riding, and that she needed to "help find a solution."[225]

The then clerk of the Privy Council, Michael Wernick, the top civil servant, was another white male in that meeting, too. He started in on his own lecture, according to Wilson-Raybould. He "made the case for the need to have a remediation agreement with SNC-Lavalin" right away because the company had a shareholders' meeting coming up and they were afraid it would decide to move its headquarters. And there was an election coming up in Quebec. As if whether the Liberal Party wins a provincial election in Quebec should be any concern of the top federal civil servant. As if any of this at all mattered to whether or not the law applied to the company or not.

These were all nonsensical excuses. The prime minister and Wernick were making up excuses to help out their criminally charged allies as a favour, and to help the party's political fortunes in Quebec. (Wernick was supposed to be a non-partisan civil servant, but it would later emerge that he had become captured by the Trudeau Liberals and had to resign over the appearance of conflict)[226] SNC-Lavalin was evidently already barred from moving its headquarters out of Montreal until at least 2024 under the terms of a loan agreement it had signed in 2017 with the Quebec public investment fund, the Caisse de dépôt et placement du Québec.[227] The head of the Caisse — which is SNC-Lavalin's largest shareholder — was already talking to SNC-Lavalin

---

225   ibid.

226   Brian Platt, "Privy Council Clerk Michael Wernick resigns after controversy over SNC-Lavalin testimony," *National Post*, March 18, 2019, *https://nationalpost. com/news/politics/privy-council-clerk-michael-wernick-resigns-after-controversy-over-snc-lavalin-testimony.*

227   Barry McKenna, "Did Trudeau fall for a bluff that SNC-Lavalin would flee Canada?" *The Globe and Mail*, Feb. 28, 2019, *https://www.theglobeandmail.com/ business/commentary/article-did-trudeau-fall-for-a-bluff-that-snc-lavalin-would-flee-canada/.*

to ensure it didn't relocate.[228, 229] And anyway, as discussed earlier, it only employs 8,500 people in Canada nowadays, less than 10 per cent of its global workforce, and far, far less than the tens of thousands of Western Canadians who had by then been put out of work in large part because of Trudeau's anti-oilpatch policies.[230] The excuse that this was about the Liberals trying to save jobs stunk from the very start.

But from that moment on, the prime minister, Wernick, Bill Morneau, Gerald Butts and others in the Prime Minister's Office and finance minister's office unleashed a relentless "gaslighting" campaign against Wilson-Raybould. Gaslighting is a term taken from a 1944 film about a man who makes his wife think she's losing her marbles by secretly moving things around and pretending it isn't happening. In this case, it was a team of men ganging up on Jody Wilson-Raybould to make her feel like she didn't understand her file. How she wasn't thinking clearly. How she wasn't informing herself properly.

It's all there in the ethics commissioner's report.[231] And it's nauseating. A group of men who claim to be Canada's greatest feminists swarming and harassing a woman of colour because she wouldn't do the unethical thing they wanted and pervert the course of justice to let a greasy Quebec company slide off the very legal hook where it had hung itself:

"Mr. Wernick testified that, according to his understanding of the law, her decision could not be final, as it was always possible for the Attorney General to receive new facts or considerations."

Ms. Wilson-Raybould brought up her concerns about Mr. Morneau's staff repeatedly speaking to her staff about SNC-Lavalin and said that it

---

228   Sandrine Rastello, "SNC-Lavalin tests largest shareholder Caisse's patience with latest profit warning, charge," *Financial Post*, July 22, 2019, *https://business.financialpost.com/news/fp-street/snc-lavalin-tests-largest-shareholder-caisses-patience-with-latest-profit-warning-charge.*

229   Dion, *Trudeau II.*

230   Tracy Johnson, "Just how many jobs have been cut in the oilpatch?," CBC News, July 6, 2016, *https://www.cbc.ca/news/canada/calgary/oil-patch-layoffs-how-many-1.3665250.*

231   Dion, *Trudeau II.*

was inappropriate. She told Mr. Morneau that his staff needed to stop contacting her office on the matter and that they were undermining the fundamental tenets of democracy and prosecutorial independence."

"Mr. Morneau did not believe Ms. Wilson-Raybould had conducted her due diligence in this matter."

Around the same time, the prime minister's senior adviser Mathieu Bouchard called Wilson-Raybould's chief of staff and "asked that Ms. Wilson-Raybould look at the option of seeking external advice with respect to the exercise of her powers under the Director of Public Prosecutions Act."

The prime minister's advisers "felt that obtaining external advice would be of assistance to the Attorney General." Which she already had done, at length — without having to be told.

In October, SNC-Lavalin's chairman Kevin Lynch — himself a former clerk of the Privy Council — talked to Scott Brison, another senior cabinet minister. "Mr. Brison stated that he believed the company's concerns appeared sensible. Following his discussion ... he contacted Ms. Wilson-Raybould that same day to bring the company's concerns to her attention." As if she hadn't already been browbeaten for weeks over those "concerns."

Bouchard later told Prince "it was fine if the Attorney General was uncomfortable intervening, but that the Prime Minister's Office did not want to close any doors on the matter ... [and] had nonetheless expressed an interest in revisiting the option of seeking external advice ... According to her notes, Mr. Bouchard stated that "we can have the best policy in the world, but we need to be re-elected."

Then in November, "Mr. Bouchard and Mr. Marques (Elder Marques, another PMO adviser) told her that if she was not sure in her decision that they could have an eminent person or panel, like Ms. McLachlin, advise her on possible options," meaning former Supreme Court chief justice Beverley McLachlin.

Wilson-Raybould "told Mr. Bouchard and Mr. Marques that they were politically interfering." But they didn't need to be told; politically interfering was exactly what they meant to do.

In December, over dinner between Butts and Wilson-Raybould, "Mr. Butts raised the idea … that the Attorney General could consider receiving an independent opinion from 'someone' like Ms. McLachlin … (and) questioned why Ms. Wilson-Raybould felt it would not be in the interest of public policy to receive independent expert advice on a new law that had never been applied before."

"According to Mr. Trudeau … Having someone respected like Ms. McLachlin would help Ms. Wilson-Raybould understand that what she was being asked to do or what it was being suggested she do was not wrong for an Attorney General."

"Mr. Butts stated that in his role as Principal Secretary, he believed it was appropriate due diligence to seek external expert advice on the matter. Based on his dinner conversation with Ms. Wilson-Raybould, Mr. Butts stated that he did not feel he had a satisfactory understanding from her on the reason she did not want to seek outside, independent advice." Even though she actually had.

Then Wernick called Wilson-Raybould and mansplained to her yet again: "The Prime Minister wants to be able to say that he has tried everything he can within the legitimate toolbox, so he is quite determined, quite firm, but he wants to know why the DPA route which Parliament provided for isn't being used. I think he's going to find a way to get it done, one way or another. So he's in that kind of a mood, and I want you to be aware of it."

And on and on, again and again, these men kept pestering the attorney general, harassing her, telling her she hadn't thought things through properly, that she wasn't doing her job properly, that she was missing some big things, that she needed advice, help, experts, more information. And what a powerful and intimidating group of political thugs these were: Not just the prime minister, the man who held the fate of her career in his hands, and his various aides, but the clerk of the Privy Council, other cabinet ministers, and the former clerk

106

of the Privy Council, Kevin Lynch. Interestingly enough, Lynch, the vice-chair at Bank of Montreal would soon see the bank hire Brison, who was on the hot seat for another scandal, the Mark Norman affair. Brison was given a plush corner-office gig.[232] Wilson-Raybould probably disqualified herself from anything like that.

And yet she endured all this pressure and condescension patiently, refusing to sacrifice what she knew was a principled position for the Liberal Party's greedy political goals.

What Wilson-Raybould didn't know was the reason that Morneau, Butts, Brison, Trudeau and his minions were all running around in full freak-out mode. It was because SNC-Lavalin was making them. The company that had called the shots from the very beginning by hatching a plot to hide in a massive omnibus budget a serious change to the Criminal Code to lessen its own punishment for alleged corruption, was getting more pushy, more demanding and more angry with the Liberals. And amazingly, the Liberals, rather than pushing back, were growing increasingly subservient. Company executives demanded more and more in-person meetings with senior Liberals — and got them. SNC-Lavalin even presented finance ministry staff a PowerPoint presentation outlining the case why it deserved a remediation agreement and told them to submit it to the prosecutors to convince them. Not only did Morneau's staff not tell the company to take a hike, they actually offered suggestions on how to improve the presentation.[233]

Yet, despite this, SNC-Lavalin kept humiliating the Liberal flunkies who were trying so hard to please them. When it finally disclosed to shareholders in October that it was not being invited to negotiate a DPA, the company's share price naturally tanked, by 14 per cent. The company forwarded an email to the Prime Minister's Office a document entitled: "SNC: Thanks for Nothing, DPPSC" (meaning

---

232   "Former Liberal cabinet minister Scott Brison joins BMO Capital Markets," *Financial Post*, Feb. 14, 2019, *https://business.financialpost.com/news/fp-street/former-liberal-cabinet-minister-scott-brison-joins-bmo-capital-markets.*

233   Dion, *Trudeau II.*

the Director of Public Prosecutions).[234] How that must have stung those Liberals who had been grovelling so long and hard to earn their parent company's affections.

Here's something else Wilson-Raybould didn't know: Those endless suggestions that she should consider meeting with someone "like" former Supreme Court chief justice McLachlin? SNC-Lavalin had already called McLachlin. It had already got her to agree to meet with Wilson-Raybould. And the company had yet another clever, devious plan. As the ethics commissioner details in his report:[235] "Ms. McLachlin would be asked to preside over a settlement conference between the Director of Public Prosecutions and SNC-Lavalin over the ongoing legal matters, and the Government of Canada could appoint Ms. McLachlin to support the negotiation of the remediation agreement."

Did you catch that? The government "could appoint Ms. McLachlin to *support* the negotiation of the remediation agreement" — added emphasis on support. They didn't just want McLachlin's neutral judgment; they were writing the verdict for her to deliver. (There is no evidence McLachlin had agreed to this.)

And McLachlin wasn't the only Supreme Court justice that SNC-Lavalin was deploying to help in the campaign to mentally break down Wilson-Raybould. They had put Frank Iacobucci on staff as legal counsel. He helpfully prepared an official legal opinion for them as to why it was right for Wilson-Raybould to intervene.[236] Then they had Iacobucci contact former Supreme Court justice John Major to provide another supportive opinion.

As the ethics commissioner would conclude, "senior staff in the Prime Minister's Office pressed Ms. Wilson-Raybould on the idea of seeking external advice on the matter—all the while knowing the advice that

---

234   ibid.

235   ibid.

236   ibid.

would be given and selectively withholding other material information from Ms. Wilson-Raybould…"[237]

The prime minister and his people were amassing all this legal advice behind Wilson-Raybould's back, while ignoring her own expert legal opinions. But not just ignoring them: Dismissing them, devaluing them, steamrolling over them. And treating her like a fool throughout, while hanging over her head the threat that her job was on the line — or, as she remembers Wernick telling her Trudeau was "going to find a way to get it done, one way or another."

And it was clear to everyone, no less Wilson-Raybould herself, that she had become a problem for the Librano family business. They realized too late she had actually come to Ottawa to "do politics differently" in deed, not just in word, as Trudeau had emptily promised. She wasn't part of the Laurentian Elite consensus — she was a West Coast Aboriginal. She didn't fit in. She actually believed in something besides corrupt power.

She was supposed to be a prop not just for Trudeau's feminism but for his "reconciliation agenda" with Aboriginals, but she wasn't supposed to actually do anything. In fact, when she had tried to involve herself in Trudeau's plans to rework Indigenous rights, he steamrolled over her then, too. She wasn't the Indian Affairs minister: That was Carolyn Bennett, a white doctor from Toronto. Why, Wilson-Raybould was just, as *National Post* columnist Kelly McParland wryly noted, not just a lawyer but "a member of the We Wai Kai First Nation, former treaty commissioner, regional chief of the B.C. Assembly of First Nations and chair of the First Nations finance authority." What could she possibly know about Indigenous rights?[238]

But then, this was the same Justin Trudeau who, having defeated Indigenous Senator Patrick Brazeau in a charity boxing match in 2012,

---

237   ibid.

238   Kelly McParland, "The Liberals think the SNC scandal is fine, and want us to vote for more of the same?" *National Post*, Aug. 19, 2019, *https://nationalpost.com/opinion/kelly-mcparland-the-liberals-think-the-snc-scandal-is-fine-and-want-us-to-vote-for-more-of-the-same.*

had taken as his prize the senator's scalp — literally chopping off the long black hair of a proud Indigenous man. Live on television. Trudeau had a tattoo of a thunderbird on his shoulder done in the style of West Coast Aboriginal art, so every white viewer must have assumed he was respectful of natives. But that was just another cultural appropriation designed to enhance his self-image. First Nations viewers instead would have recognized the ghastly symbolism of a white French-Canadian chopping off the thick mane of an Aboriginal man. As Clayton Thomas-Muller, a member of Manitoba's Pukatawagan First Nation, and a writer, would later despair: "What possessed Trudeau to think, in a time of residential school apologies and moves towards reconciliation, that the public shaming of a First Nations man was appropriate or empowering? Was the fight some sort of rite of passage for an uncrowned prince?"[239]

Clayton-Muller couldn't help but note that not long after, Brazeau's self-destructive spiral of run-ins with the law and public drunkenness deepened badly, culminating in an unsuccessful suicide attempt.[240] "Allegations of sexual harassment and public drunkenness were already dogging the senator when he stepped into the ring, but to this day I wonder how much the symbolism of cutting off Brazeau's hair, no less in the halls of the settler-colonial state of Canada, sent that pitiful man on his final spiral."

And then in March 2019, when Trudeau was speaking at a Liberal fundraiser in Toronto, he was confronted by protestors from the Ontario First Nations communities of Grassy Narrows and Wabaseemoong. They were trying to draw his attention to a crisis of mercury poison in their water. Because the fundraiser was exclusively attended by Laurier Club members — a VIP circle of members who give at least $1,500 a year to the party — Trudeau had only one, incredibly smug remark for these suffering Aboriginals: "Thank you very much for your donation

239   Clayton Thomas-Muller, "Trudeau is no friend to First Nations," Ricochet, Sept. 24, 2015, *https://ricochet.media/en/613/trudeau-is-no-friend-to-first-nations.*

240   Gary Dimmock, "Senator Brazeau's darkest hour: 'I let a lot of people down'," *Ottawa Citizen,* June 26, 2018, *https://ottawacitizen.com/news/national/0514-pb.*

tonight, I really appreciate it," he repeatedly said, as the protestors were marched out of the room by his bodyguards. And his audience, full of sycophantic fans, cheered and applauded.

This was the real Trudeau: a poser who used fake words to delude people into thinking he respected women and who sported a culturally-appropriated First Nations tattoo to delude people into thinking he cared about Aboriginals. When he was finally confronted with a proud, competent, principled and courageous Aboriginal woman who would not follow his unethical orders, he sought to answer her impudence with deceit and attempts to humiliate her. He bullied her. He threatened her. And eventually he punished her: Demoting her from justice minister and attorney general to minister of veterans affairs.

But even then, she outsmarted him.

On Feb. 7, 2019, *The Globe and Mail* broke the story that the Prime Minister's Office had inappropriately pressured Wilson-Raybould on the SNC-Lavalin file. Trudeau and his people naturally lied and said the story was untrue. Ten days later he tried using the excuse that because Wilson-Raybould remained in cabinet, it was proof she still supported him. The next day, on February 12, Wilson-Raybould resigned from cabinet.[241] It was glorious.

The prime minister tried to fight back. He tried to demean her publicly. He had his pink-shirted feminist shock troops start leaking to the media that she was "difficult to get along with," was "known to berate fellow cabinet ministers openly at the table," and someone who "others felt they had trouble trusting."[242] He even tried smearing her integrity for daring to protect herself by recording one of the conversations in which Wernick had delivered the ominous message about how the

---

241   Amanda Connolly, "Jody Wilson-Raybould resigns from cabinet amid SNC-Lavalin affair, Trudeau 'surprised and disappointed'," Global News, Feb. 12, 2019, *https://globalnews.ca/news/4952236/jody-wilson-raybould-resigns-snc-lavalin-affair/.*

242   Mia Rabson, "Wilson-Raybould entered federal politics hoping to be a bridge builder," *National Post*, Feb. 9, 2019, *https://nationalpost.com/pmn/news-pmn/canada-news-pmn/wilson-raybould-entered-federal-politics-hoping-to-be-a-bridge-builder.*

prime minister was going to "get it done one way or other," calling it "unconscionable."[243]

Trudeau's message was unmistakable: See how these Aboriginal women can get too big for their britches? Trudeau deliberately called her by her first name "Jody" whenever he spoke publicly about her, a sign of blatant disrespect for an accomplished former Crown prosecutor and cabinet minister.[244] And she, all the while, had to hold her tongue — had to stay quiet due to cabinet confidences and the duty of maintain the privilege between the government and the (now former) attorney general.

But Wilson-Raybould was shortly joined by Jane Philpott, a highly accomplished and highly respected cabinet minister who was appalled at what she had seen in Wilson-Raybould's treatment. On March 4, Philpott issued a statement explaining that she had lost faith in the prime minister and his cabinet:[245]

"In Canada, the constitutional convention of Cabinet solidarity means, among other things, that ministers are expected to defend all Cabinet decisions. A minister must always be prepared to defend other ministers publicly, and must speak in support of the government and its policies. Given this convention and the current circumstances, it is untenable for me to continue to serve as a Cabinet minister.

"Unfortunately, the evidence of efforts by politicians and/or officials to pressure the former Attorney General to intervene in the criminal case involving SNC-Lavalin, and the evidence as to the content of those efforts have raised serious concerns for me. Those concerns have

243   Kathleen Harris, "Trudeau ejects Wilson-Raybould, Philpott from Liberal caucus," CBC News, April 2, 2019, *https://www.cbc.ca/news/politics/liberals-wilson-raybould-philpott-caucus-1.5080880.*

244   Candice Malcolm, "Trudeau's fake feminism has now been exposed," *Toronto Sun*, Feb. 13, 2019, *https://torontosun.com/opinion/columnists/malcolm-trudeaus-fake-feminism-has-now-been-exposed.*

245   "Jane Philpott resigns from cabinet: Full statement," *Maclean's*, March 4, 2019, *https://www.macleans.ca/politics/ottawa/jane-philpott-resigns-from-cabinet-full-statement/.*

been augmented by the views expressed by my constituents and other Canadians.

"The solemn principles at stake are the independence and integrity of our justice system. It is a fundamental doctrine of the rule of law that our Attorney General should not be subjected to political pressure or interference regarding the exercise of her prosecutorial discretion in criminal cases. Sadly, I have lost confidence in how the government has dealt with this matter and in how it has responded to the issues raised."

Over the following weeks, Wilson-Raybould would be called to testify about the allegations of interference at the House standing committee on ethics. Her testimony would result in the resignation of Gerald Butts as the prime minister's principal secretary.[246] The testimony of the clerk of the Privy Council, Michael Wernick, was so unhinged (he predicted "someone is going to be shot" because of the anger over the scandal) and so biased (he insisted the Liberals, "always conducted themselves to the highest standards of integrity," despite their many proven ethical violations), that he too was forced to step down over appearing too partisan.[247]

Wilson-Raybould had laid waste to Trudeau's reputation and to his team.

On April 2, 2019, he finally threw her and Philpott out of the Liberal caucus. It was all that was left for him to do.

Just over four months later, the ethics commissioner would deliver his bombshell report called *Trudeau II*. And the sequel, just like the original, would find that the Liberal prime minister had broken federal law. Again.

---

246   John Paul Tasker, "Gerald Butts resigns as Prime Minister Justin Trudeau's principal secretary," CBC News, Feb. 18, 2019, *https://www.cbc.ca/news/politics/ gerald-butts-resigns-pmo-1.5023675.*

247   David Akin, "An absurd, fascinating, partisan and remarkably helpful tale on Trudeau and SNC-Lavalin," Global News, Feb. 22, 2019, *https://globalnews.ca/ news/4989095/clerk-privy-council-michael-wernick/.*

Ethics Commissioner Mario Dion had focused this time on Section 9 of the Conflict of Interest Act, which reads: "No public office holder shall use his or her position as a public office holder to seek to influence a decision of another person so as to further the public office holder's private interests or those of the public office holder's relatives or friends or to improperly further another person's private interests."[248]

That Trudeau had done just that was inescapable, he concluded. Trudeau had "used his position of authority over Ms. Wilson-Raybould to seek to influence her decision on whether she should overrule the Director of Public Prosecutions' decision not to invite SNC-Lavalin to enter into negotiations towards a remediation agreement." He was doing so to benefit himself, and his party, electorally, but also to further the private interests of his corporate-sector friends at SNC-Lavalin, concluded Dion.[249]

"For these reasons, I find that Mr. Trudeau contravened section 9 of the Act."

---

248   Conflict of Interest Act, Part 1, *https://laws-lois.justice.gc.ca/eng/acts/C-36.65/page-2.html#h-92089*.

249   Dion, *Trudeau II*.

CHAPTER 10

FRIENDS AND ENEMIES

In 2005, a long-haired, blue-jeaned 33-year-old Justin Trudeau told an audience of Ottawa high-school students that it would be a long time before he possessed the proper judgment to use his father's famous name for the benefit of the Canadian people. "I tell you right now I'd make a lousy political figure," he told them in a speech where he had come to talk about Katimavik, the national youth service organization that he was chairing, which was started by his father's government. "I'm a long way from being able to wield the power that would come with my name to purely good effect," Trudeau said.[250]

Three years later he was an MP.

Eight years later he was leader of the Liberals.

Less than 10 years later, he was prime minister.

Somewhere along the way, Trudeau's lust for fame and power evidently grew more important than his need to use the strength of his last name "to purely good effect." As the leader of the Canadian government, he

---

250   Patricia Sherlock, "Justin Trudeau says he's not ready for politics — yet," *Ottawa Citizen*, March 10, 2005.

would still have the power of that name, of course; but the effect he would use it for would be for entirely different reasons than the purely good.

Because if there's anything that the SNC-Lavalin scandal shows, it's that the Libranos under Justin Trudeau will stop at nothing to do nasty things, if that's what helping out the party or its friends requires.

No matter how corrupt those friends may be. No matter how dirty the deeds required. If breaking the law in an attempt to attack the heart of the independence of the Canadian judicial system is called for, Trudeau won't flinch. Since the ethics commissioner's report, the Conservative party has even called for the RCMP to investigate whether the actions of the prime minister and his henchmen constituted a criminal offence: Section 139 of the Criminal Code that makes it illegal to "obstruct, pervert or defeat the course of justice."[251]

And if there's another thing that this shocking and disgraceful scandal shows, it's that there's virtually nothing that Trudeau and his goons won't do to destroy an enemy.

Together, they expose yet another fake side of the carefully concocted image of Trudeau: That he's a man of morals.

Trudeau has presented himself to the world as compassionate, caring and considerate. That he cares for the downtrodden. That he seeks justice for the world. But that too is a fraud. Trudeau's moral compass does not point towards mercy and justice. Its magnetic north is one of self-interest, power, domination and cruelty.

His attempts to humiliate Jody Wilson-Raybould and to spread malicious gossip about her was not the last time he would try to literally ruin someone who dared to challenge his power.

---

251   Amanda Connolly, "Scheer requests RCMP probe on Trudeau's SNC-Lavalin interference," Global News, Aug. 19, 2019, *https://globalnews.ca/ news/5782954/snc-lavalin-rcmp-scheer-probe/*.

Former Vice-Admiral Mark Norman had his career destroyed and his life devastated for years after he somehow, even indirectly, angered the vindictive and merciless prime minister.

Norman was a highly decorated soldier who had earned every bar on his sleeve and medal on his chest after working his way up from a Navy mechanic to vice-chief of the defence staff. That was until a CBC reporter was leaked a story that Trudeau did not want leaked. There was no proof the story was leaked by Norman; in fact, another public service employee was later charged with leaking and it turned out that many people were aware of the information that was leaked and could have been behind it. The information wasn't even a matter of national security: The information that the CBC reported was that the Trudeau cabinet was considering putting on hold an important contract assigned by the Harper government to Davie Shipbuilding to quickly retrofit a supply ship — a fire had disabled the Navy's last one. (A supply ship is like a floating gas station, able to provide gunships with fuel and supplies at sea). The Irving family, a rival shipbuilder with close ties to Liberals including Scott Brison (and Dominic LeBlanc) had never liked the award, which had been hurriedly sole-sourced for urgency's sake . So the Liberals were thinking of stopping the whole thing in its tracks, leaving the Navy without a supply ship for who knows how long.

And then the story, by the CBC James Cudmore, leaked. The Liberals were too embarrassed then to change the contract. (The ship ultimately came in on time and under budget.[252]) And Trudeau was furious. He set his sights on one man: Vice-Admiral Norman. And he set out to destroy him.

Trudeau asked the RCMP to investigate. Soon after, Norman was abruptly suspended from his job. Mounties raided his home and confiscated his computers and other personal property. It took over a year for him to be charged with anything, but that didn't stop the

---

252   Christie Blatchford, "Canadian military has bigger problems beyond the curse of sexual misconduct," *National Post*, May 22, 2019, *https://nationalpost.com/opinion/christie-blatchford-canadian-military-has-bigger-problems-beyond-the-curse-of-sexual-misconduct.*

prime minister from publicly declaring his certainty that Norman would be tried for crimes. Three months after Norman was suspended, when asked about the strange suspension of Mark Norman, Trudeau answered: "This is an important matter that is obviously under investigation, and will likely end up before the courts, so I won't make any further comments at this time." But how could he know that? That was roughly a year before any charge would be laid. How could he predict that an investigation for which no charges had yet been laid would "likely end up before the courts"? Unless, as with the SNC-Lavalin affair, he had his political fingers meddling in the case itself.[253]

Nearly a year later, Norman had still not been charged, and had been stuck in a strange legal limbo while the Crown evidently tried to put some kind of case together against him. And yet, Trudeau was predicting again how the investigation would turn out and that Norman would be charged and tried. This time, Trudeau didn't say it would "likely" end up in court; when a citizen asked him about the apparent "witch hunt" against Norman at a Town Hall in Edmonton, this time said he couldn't comment because the case would "inevitably" go to court. Again, this was before a single charge had even been laid against Norman. A month later, the RCMP finally charged Norman with one count of breach of trust.[254]

When Norman applied for a special fund that provides public service employees loans to defend themselves against charges — repayable if the charges stick — he was cruelly denied even that, leaving him to face hundreds of thousands of legal costs on his own. Why? Because the Department of Defence said he was guilty. It had already decided the fate of his case, before he was even convicted![255] The government

---

253 David Pugliese, "'The fight of your life': In a Postmedia exclusive, Mark Norman tells his side of the story," *National Post*, May 17, 2019, *https://nationalpost. com/news/politics/the-fight-of-your-life-in-a-postmedia-exclusive-mark-norman-tells-his-side-of-the-story*.

254 ibid.

255 David Pugliese, "No charges, no investigation — but DND declares Vice-Admiral Mark Norman is guilty," *National Post,* Jan. 22, 2018, *https://nationalpost. com/news/politics/mark-norman-one-of-only-three-people-dnd-refused-to-give-help-with-legal-bills-in-past-two-years*.

refused to hand over documents to Norman's defence team and even used secret code words rather than Norman's name to elude any requests for other documents related to the case.

The Liberals even hired Cudmore, the same CBC reporter who was the first to expose the leak, as a senior adviser in the defence ministry, no doubt hoping to use his knowledge of the original source against the vice-admiral. (Brison, meanwhile, no doubt nervous about what details the trial would reveal, skedaddled out of politics and took that cushy executive Bank of Montreal job with Kevin Lynch, who had called on Brison's helpful cabinet-minister services in Lynch's capacity as SNC-Lavalin chairman.)

Mark Norman was up against the full force of the Trudeau government. And he paid dearly for it.

Until the case fell completely apart. In fact, there never was a case. The government, it turned out, had not even bothered to interview important potential witnesses who had worked with the former Harper government, witnesses who eventually gave the defence what it needed to expose the case as a fraud. The Liberals had faked and deceived and manipulated a single man's life and career for as long as they could. Until they could wring him dry no longer. And then they just walked away.[256]

Norman's lawyer, the star defender Marie Henein, essentially accused the government of another dirty attempt to meddle in Canada's independent judicial system. She said the Prime Minister's Office and the Privy Council were "counselling witnesses as to what they could and could not say," in addition to hiding and withholding evidence. "No person in this country should ever walk into a courtroom and feel like they're fighting their elected government," she said. "What you

---

256   Pugliese, "The fight."

don't do, is you don't is put your finger and try to weigh in on the scales of justice."[257]

Norman was left to negotiate a settlement and, having been smeared and denigrated by the very establishment he had served for 39 years, could not return to the Navy. He quietly took his retirement and went about trying to put his life back together.

They say you can judge a man by the quality of his enemies. The remarkable truth that had become clear about Trudeau was that he was turning into enemies the most principled, respected, hard-working Canadian public servants: former Crown prosecutor Wilson-Raybould; former Air Force captain Leona Alleslev; Jane Philpott, a doctor who once moved to Africa to train medical workers; former vice-admiral Norman.

His list of friends, meanwhile, not only included a company blacklisted around the world for its corrupt practices and facing charges in Canada for its cosiness with a monstrous Middle East dictatorship. A more thorough look at who Trudeau supports and has helped gain advantage and power in Canada reveals a long list of those who work relentlessly to undermine Canadian values.

Remember when Trudeau said he admired Communist China because he saw their dictatorship as better than democracy? At a 2013 Toronto fundraiser, he actually said: "There's a level of admiration I actually have for China because their basic dictatorship is allowing them to actually turn their economy around on a dime and say, 'We need to go green ... we need to start investing in solar.'"[258] Oh, that would be that admirable dictatorship that millions of people in Hong Kong for months in 2019 have been desperately protesting to avoid being swallowed up by. The admirable dictatorship that can turn around on

---

257   Jason Unrau, "Norman's lawyer alleges Trudeau government counselled witnesses, has not ruled out civil suit," *Post Millennial*, May 8, 2019, *https://www.thepostmillennial.com/normans-lawyer-speaks-out-on-political-interference-has-not-ruled-out-civil-suit-against-trudeau-government/*.

258   "Trudeau under fire for expressing admiration for China's 'basic dictatorship'," CTV News, Nov. 8, 2013, *https://www.ctvnews.ca/politics/trudeau-under-fire-for-expressing-admiration-for-china-s-basic-dictatorship-1.1535116*.

a dime and round up a million Uighur Muslims and lock them into "re-education" camps where they're forced to disavow their religion. The admirable dictatorship that can turn on a dime and kidnap two innocent Canadians because it's mad at us for executing an arrest warrant on one of their favourite business executives. That admirable dictatorship. Well, it also turns out that admirable dictatorship is actually building far more coal power plants than it is solar farms.[259]

In retrospect, that wasn't just an idiotic attempt at trying to imitate the mediocre thinking of a community college professor. It would turn out to be one of the most revealing clues about Trudeau's true feelings about how he wishes government would work: He doesn't actually like democracy. He hates accountability. He wants to change things his way, and help his causes and his friends, and becomes enraged when anyone — attorney generals, loyal military officers, anyone — gets in his way.

It isn't just China. Trudeau was hosting a night on Broadway for diplomats in New York for the UN Conference in 2017. Trudeau bought out the entire theatre, for $30,000. But along with Canadian lawyers and lobbyists, there was no tyranny in the world Trudeau did not invite that night: He invited leaders from Cuba, China, Venezuela, Burma. OPEC and terrorist countries. And countries with whom Canada even has sanctions in place, like Iran. He was clearly bribing every scumbag at the UN, because he wants Canada to have a seat on the security council (a seat Canada lost because former prime minister Harper refused to suck up to those same lowlifes).[260]

Besides, Trudeau doesn't have the same anti-terrorist feelings as most Canadians do. Remember how after the Boston Marathon terror bombing he blamed it on North American society, rather than Islamic extremism, saying "there is no question that this happened because

---

259   Steve Inskeep, "Why Is China Placing A Global Bet On Coal?" NPR, April 29, 2019, *https://www.npr.org/2019/04/29/716347646/why-is-china-placing-a-global-bet-on-coal.*

260   Ezra Levant, "To get back UN seat, Trudeau bribes dictators — with Broadway tickets," Rebel Media, May 12, 2017, *https://www.therebel.media/ezra_levant_may_12_2017.*

there is someone who feels completely excluded."[261] Well, since then, he arranged for the government to apologize to and reward Omar Khadr to the tune of $10.5 million. Khadr, the son of Canada's "first family of terror," linked not only to the murderous al-Qaida terror cult but to its infamous former leader, Osama bin Laden, himself — they were family friends.[262] Khadr who killed an American medic in Afghanistan, as he fought against Canadian and allied troops. Trudeau handed him $10.5 million as compensation for having been caught on the battlefield and held in Guantanamo Bay, rather than being brought back to Canada. [263] And Trudeau apologized to him — something he's never done to Wilson-Raybould, Norman, or any of the other upstanding, loyal Canadians he's tried to personally ruin.

Khadr isn't the only dangerous Islamic radical Trudeau has a soft spot for. When Canadian Joshua Boyle returned from Afghanistan in 2017, after being radicalized and then held captive there, Trudeau even hosted him for a pre-Christmas get-together at his office on Parliament Hill. Two weeks later, Boyle was charged with 19 crimes including assault, sexual assault and forcible confinement. (He has pleaded not guilty).[264]

And Trudeau actually promotes the idea of bringing even more terrorists home to Canada, with who knows how much taxpayer money to help them. He has said he wants to bring home Canadians who left the country to go join and fight with the monstrous Islamic State in Syria or Iraq (ISIL). That's the group that beheads people on YouTube and captures little girls as sex slaves, among other gross and

---

261   "Don't 'sit around trying to rationalize it': Harper slams Trudeau for response to Boston bombing," *National Post*, April 17, 2013, *https://nationalpost.com/ news/politics/trudeaus-response-to-boston-marathon-bombing-was-unacceptable-made-excuses-for-terrorists-harper-says.*

262   "Key events in the Omar Khadr case," CBC News, Sept. 30, 2012, *https:// www.cbc.ca/news/canada/key-events-in-the-omar-khadr-case-1.1153759.*

263   Colin Perkel, "U.S. plaintiffs fire back at Khadr defence over damages-award enforcement," CBC News, Jan. 11, 2018, *https://www.cbc.ca/news/politics/ plaintiffs-attack-khadr-defence-damages-1.4483092.*

264   "Here is what you need to know about the timeline of events for Joshua Boyle and Caitlan Coleman," Global News, March 27, 2019, *https://globalnews.ca/ news/5101139/joshua-boyle-caitlan-coleman-timeline/.*

violent crimes. He said they might prove to be a "powerful voice for preventing radicalization," if they have "turned away" from their hateful, murderous ideology. As for those who bring their hateful, murderous ideology with them back home, well, Trudeau evidently figures we'll just have to learn to live with them living in our neighbourhoods.[265]

Trudeau's tolerance for radicals is of a piece with his admiration for dictatorships. In both cases, he seems to have a disturbing tolerance for extreme, dominating anti-democratic movements that are willing to use violence if necessary to achieve power over the popular will. It's as much there in his admiration for communists and his compassion for terrorists as it is in his support for extremist environmental groups. These are groups that have no interest in the prosperity of Canada — their ambiguous missions to preserve the environment or stop climate change are necessarily global in nature. By their nature, they transcend national interests and so they end up in opposition to the popular will of democracies like Canada. Their means can only be achieved by capturing compliant politicians. They managed it for a while in Ontario with Dalton McGuinty and Kathleen Wynne, before those Liberal leaders were thrown out of office by voters fed up with their costly, economically destructive quest to win the green seal of approval from globalist environmentalists. They managed it for a few years in Alberta, until the NDP was thrown out after one term, largely over its carbon-taxing anti-oil policies. And they did it for a while in the U.S. with the Obama administration, until Americans voted in a president willing to cancel the entire green charade, start approving more pipelines and more drilling, and pulled America out of the Paris climate accord.

But no government in the world has been captured by extremist environmentalists as this one has. Gerald Butts, the former principal adviser to the prime minister, had moved from the McGuinty administration to running the anti-fossil-fuel World Wildlife Fund, and then straight into the prime minister's office. On his way out the

---

265   Roy Green, "Trudeau's troubling take on returning ISIS fighters," Global News, Dec. 27, 2017, *https://globalnews.ca/news/3935427/roy-green-trudeaus-troubling-take-on-returning-isis-fighters/*.

door, the WWF even paid him over $360,000 as a "severance" — even though he was resigning, not being let go — ensuring he would remain loyal to their cause.[266]

And boy was he ever. Butts set about staffing the government of a heavily resource-based economy with the most anti-resource activists he could find. The list of anti-oil warriors Butts seeded among the top ranks of the Canadian government is as breathtaking as it is scandalous:[267] Sarah Goodman, formerly of the extremist anti-Alberta-oil group Tides Canada, was made a policy director in the Prime Minister's Office; Marlo Raynolds, formerly of the environmental group Pembina Institute was made chief of staff to Environment Minister Catherine McKenna; Erin Flanagan, formerly of Pembina, was made policy director to minister of natural resources, Jim Carr; Zoe Caron, formerly of the World Wildlife Fund and the Sierra Club, was put on staff at the Prime Minister's Office and worked as chief of staff to the minister of natural resources; Steven Guilbeault, a staunch opponent of pipelines from the hardcore group Equiterre was made co-chair on the government's Advisory Panel on Climate Action and has now been recruited to run for the Liberals in 2019; and there's many more. And the result has been exactly what Butts has been working for: The gradual destruction of Alberta's economically vital oil and gas industry. Investors walking away from two pipelines — Energy East and Trans Mountain — after endless delays, and an outright ban on a third, Northern Gateway, and a further ban on any Alberta oil being exported at all from Northern B.C. Oh, and those tens of thousands of Canadian workers thrown out of work by Liberal policies — even as the Liberals lied about how doing SNC-Lavalin's dirty work was all about wanting to protect "Canadian jobs."

266   Vivian Krause, "The Political Activity Audits of Charities: Fair Questions for the CRA," Fair Questions blog, April 16, 2018, *https://fairquestions.typepad.com/ rethink_campaigns/2018/04/fair-questions-for-the-cra-part-1.html.*

267   Gwyn Morgan, "Talk about 'collusion': How foreign-backed anti-oil activists infiltrated Canada's government," *Financial Post*, March 14, 2019, *https:// business.financialpost.com/opinion/gwyn-morgan-talk-about-collusion-how-foreign-backed-anti-oil-activists-infiltrated-canadas-government.*

In only a few short years, Trudeau has praised those, like China, who are fighting to upend the entire liberal world order. He has embraced terrorists and their supporters who are at war with western society. And he has empowered the anti-democratic environmental extremists determined to sap Canada's economic strength. And all the while he has only alienated and angered longtime allies, former friends and loyal Canadians.

Less than six months after Canadians learned the shocking news that Trudeau would pay the terrorist Omar Khadr $10.5 million, he was confronted by Brock Blaszczyk, an Afghan veteran at a Town Hall event in Edmonton. Trudeau's government had literally been fighting injured veterans in court to deny them disability payments. Blaszczyk had lost his leg in an explosion serving Canada in the fight against terrorists like Khadr. And Trudeau had the gall to tell him it was because veterans were asking "for more than we can give right now."[268]

Trudeau had millions to give Khadr; but disability payments for men and women injured serving their country? That just wasn't something Trudeau could see spending money on. This from a prime minister who has run up more than $300 billion in new debt since taking office.[269] Not because there was an urgent need to spend: His term coincided with steady economic growth and low unemployment. But because he felt like spending. He just didn't feel like spending on injured soldiers.

And while Trudeau was turning his back on loyal Canadian servicemen here at home, he was also turning it on longtime allies. Most notably, Trudeau has repeatedly taunted our longtime ally and most-important trading partner, the United States. When Donald Trump was elected president in November 2016, Trudeau didn't feel like adapting the relationship to a new American direction and tone. Instead, he used

268   Emma Graney, "Justin Trudeau quizzed by sometimes testy audience at Edmonton town hall," *Edmonton Journal*, Feb. 2, 2018, *https://edmontonjournal.com/news/politics/prime-minister-justin-trudeau-to-speak-in-edmonton.*

269   Jake Fuss, Finn Poschmann and Milagros Palacioas, "Prime Minister Trudeau cements his 'debt' legacy," Fraser Institute, April 29, 2019, *https://www.fraserinstitute.org/article/prime-minister-trudeau-cements-his-debt-legacy.*

it as an opportunity to enhance his own phony brand of compassion, tolerance and global responsibility by denigrating Trump.

Much of Trudeau's foreign policy seems to be like the child's game, Simon Says — but the opposite. Whatever Trump decides to do, Trudeau will simply do or say the opposite. Trump brought in tougher immigration rules from several terrorist-dominated countries; Trudeau immediately tweeted that everyone is welcome in Canada. Trump cut off hundreds of millions of dollars in foreign aid to the Gaza Strip, a Palestinian territory dominated by the Hamas terrorist group; in reaction, Trudeau jacked up Canada's own foreign aid there. Trump got tough with Cuba; Trudeau visited and praised the prison island.

Trudeau's foreign policy hasn't just been anti-American. It's been amateurish and narcissistic.

Take Trudeau's bizarre personal conduct at negotiations for the Trans Pacific Partnership, a controversial trade treaty made up of several developing Asian countries. First he infuriated them by boycotting a November 10, 2017 meeting, drawing accusations from some foreigners that he was "sabotaging" the deal.[270] He angered Japan, one of the TPP partners, by continuing to ask for vague improvements to the deal, without specifying what they were, which "grated on Japanese sensitivities," according to one well-placed former diplomat. He had reportedly "upset" the Japanese president specifically. "Prime Minister Trudeau said, 'No, no, we cannot get on board. We still have problems.' And what is the problem? There was no clear answer," said the director of Japan's business federation.[271] Oh well, Japan is only the third-largest economy in the world. Who really cares if we get a trade

---

270   Stuart Thomson, "Justin Trudeau accused of 'sabotaging' trade deal with meeting no-show," *National Post*, Nov. 10, 2017, *https://nationalpost.com/news/politics/justin-trudeau-accused-of-sabotaging-trade-deal-and-infuriating-world-leaders-with-meeting-no-show.*

271   Marie-Danielle Smith, "'We don't know what Canada wants': Japanese chorus of confusion grows over Trudeau's TPP position," *National Post*, Dec. 21, 2017, *https://nationalpost.com/news/politics/we-dont-know-what-canada-wants-japanese-chorus-of-confusion-grows-over-trudeaus-tpp-position.*

deal with them, not to mention the nine other countries in the TPP? (The treaty was eventually signed in 2018.)

But worse than all that has been his treatment of India, the world's-largest democracy and a friend of Canadian interests as a moderating force in a restive and dangerous region that includes Afghanistan and Pakistan.

In February 2018, Trudeau took his wife and kids to India on what was supposed to be a friendship and trade mission but was revealed to be a lightly scheduled family vacation so obnoxious in its cultural insensitivity that even the editorialists at the Liberal-loving *Toronto Star* were forced to grimly judge it "the least successful foray into that country since the repelled Mongol invasions."[272] He pranced around the country wearing local costumes like a backpacking university student who had decided to go native. He banghra danced badly onstage like a Bollywood wannabe. He greeted Indian celebrities who wore dapper business suits while he, in his sherwani, bowed with his hands folded like he was imitating Mike Myers in the slapstick comedy, *The Love Guru*.

And yet, when it came to actually experiencing true Indian culture, Trudeau preferred to stick with his more upper-class colonialist ways, bringing with him his own chef, Vikram Vij, from Vancouver, to prepare supposedly "authentic" Indian cuisine, at an added cost of $17,000. The opposition pointed out that there were plenty of local cooks who knew how to do Indian cuisine just as well, who didn't require plane fare.[273]

It was a $1.5-million family trip that Trudeau had stuck Canadians with for no discernible reason. No deals were made. The Indian prime minister, Narendra Modi, didn't bother to meet with Trudeau until his

---

272   "Justin Trudeau's very bad trip to India may carry a steep cost," *Toronto Star*, Feb. 22, 2018, *https://www.thestar.com/opinion/editorials/2018/02/22/justin-trudeaus-very-bad-trip-to-india-may-carry-a-steep-cost.html.*

273   John Ivison, *Trudeau: The Education of a Prime Minister* (Toronto; Signal), 2019, p. 228.

last day of the visit.[274] But there was good reason for that: Trudeau had invited a terrorist Sikh separatist convicted of attempting to murder an Indian politician to an exclusive dinner with him at the Canadian High Commissioner's residence in New Delhi. Modi naturally raised the problem in his brief meeting, reminding Trudeau "there should be no space for those who seek to divide communities and promote separatism. We will not tolerate those who challenge unity and integrity of our countries."

The terrorist incident was the lowest-light of what had been a public-relations catastrophe for the Trudeau government from the moment the preening prime minister set foot on Indian soil. But rather than being humbled and apologetic about it, the Liberals did what they always do: They blamed someone else. In this case, they actually blamed the Indian government for their own calamitous screw up. Gerald Butts, the prime minister's top adviser, told the *National Post*'s John Ivison his paranoid conspiracy theory that conservatives were working together to help humiliate the Liberals, and had set a trap. "We walked into a buzzsaw," he said. "Modi and his government were out to screw us and were throwing tacks under our tires to help Canadian conservatives, who did a good job of embarrassing us."[275]

Of course Trudeau and his people hadn't been to blame for the disaster that was that ill-conceived, overpriced vanity trip that ended in scandal. That's the great thing about being a Librano: The charges never stick.

---

274   Steve George and Huizhong Wu, "Trudeau's trip, mired in controversy, ends in a hug," Feb. 23, 2018, *https://www.cnn.com/2018/02/23/asia/india-trudeau-modi-hug-intl/index.html*.

275   Ivison, *Trudeau*. p. 228.

CHAPTER 11

WE'VE GOT TO KICK THEM OUT

It took Trudeau's garish, tasteless and self-indulgent India trip to tip the scales among Canadians who had overlooked so much of his vain and conceited behaviour before. It was so over the top, such a repugnant display by a man who sought endless publicity for himself so desperate was he for the endless approval of social media, that the Canadian stomach finally began to turn. His addiction to photos of himself, which had once charmed Canadians, had, with such a vulgar show of dress-up and showboating, finally begun to repulse them. Within just a couple of weeks, the polls turned badly against Trudeau, actually putting them behind the Tories for the first time since Trudeau's election. The honeymoon was officially over.[276]

But what it revealed was what close watchers had seen all along: A man who was in government all for himself — for his own aggrandizement, for his own vanity, for his own pet causes, for his own friends, and,

---

276   Amanda Connolly, "Justin Trudeau would lose if an election were held tomorrow, India trip a symptom of shift in mood: Ipsos poll," Global News, March 2, 2018, *https://globalnews.ca/news/4058984/justin-trudeau-india-trip-ipsos-poll/*.

above all, for his own material benefit. After all, what good is it being the boss of the Libranos, if you can't live like a king?

The million-and-a-half-dollar Trudeau family vacation to India struck Canadians as an obnoxious waste, given its lack of substance, and worse, the fact that it set back Indo-Canadian relations by a decade or more, thanks to the Liberals' cringeworthy bungling. But it also happened to occur just a few weeks after the ethics and conflict of interest commissioner had delivered the first report that would find Trudeau guilty of breaking the law, this time over his family's private helicopter trips to Billionaire Lobbyist Tropical Vacation Island. Now, Canadians were starting to get the picture: Trudeau wasn't just raising taxes and running up eye-watering debts, so he could spend more on the government. He was certainly doing that. But he and his fellow Libranos were also helping themselves with both hands to every luxury and perk they could.

The first clue about that should have been more obvious. It came in the first year of Trudeau's term: Two of his most senior advisers at the time, Gerald Butts and Katie Telford, tried to get away with charging taxpayers more than $200,000 in expenses because they moved from Toronto to Ottawa to work for Trudeau.[277] A four-hour drive away and they wanted two-hundred-grand in compensation. And amazingly, Trudeau had approved it.

It was robbery in broad daylight. They hadn't just charged for moving expenses and realtors' fees (despite the fact that they probably pocketed a fortune in what was then a red-hot Toronto real-estate market). Telford claimed an implausible $23,373 for a "personalized cash payout and incidentals." Butts, who had just pocketed nearly four-hundred grand for quitting the World Wildlife Fund to go work for Trudeau, claimed $20,700 for the same shady reasons, and another $18,247 for "temporary accommodations" while he was moving. That was on top of Butts's apparently wildly inflated claim for "land transfer tax, legal fees and insurance" for over $25,000. Even Telford

---

277   Peter Zimonjic, "Senior PMO staffers Gerald Butts and Katie Telford to return $65K in 'unreasonable' moving expenses," CBC News, Sept. 22, 2016, *https://www.cbc.ca/news/politics/butts-telford-moving-expenses-1.3774979.*

had claimed nothing like that. Butts later had to admit the figure was "over and above what would have been the cost of the tax on a home at the average house price in Ottawa for 2016." So he was just expensing as much as he could. Between his approaching half-a-million-dollar WWF payout, his six-figure moving expenses, and actually getting a severance package after he resigned from the Prime Minister's Office in the SNC-Lavalin scandal in 2019, Butts may have earned enough to retire after just three years working in government![278]

It took the public embarrassment of media reports for Butts and Telford to finally agree to pay back a portion of the money — $65,000 of the two-hundred grand — admitting they had made unreasonable claims. But they paid no other price. Trudeau refused to punish them for literally trying to claim expenses for more than they were properly owed. In any other corporation, embezzlement or filing false expense claims would be answered with a swift dismissal and possibly criminal charges. For the Libranos, it's a way of doing business. And everyone around Trudeau — from other cabinet ministers, to junior staff, to civil servants — saw it. The boss and his right hand man are grifting as hard as they can, stuffing their pockets with whatever they can. That's the culture at the top — you can bet the lesson has been learned by everyone below.

But none of them exemplifies that as much as Justin Trudeau does. He spends public money lavishly on himself, as if being prime minister were the same as winning Lotto 6/49. He hired not one, but two nannies to work in his house, paid for by taxpayers.[279] This despite the fact that Sophie is a stay-at-home mom and Trudeau himself takes an average of several "personal days" or "vacation days" every month. He actually somehow managed to take 10 vacations in his first year as prime minister. Ten! He flew off to tropical St. Kitts, went skiing in Whistler, celebrated Carnaval in Quebec, chilled at an exclusive resort

---

278   Charlie Pinkerton, "Butts entitled to severance despite resigning from PMO," iPolitics, Feb. 25, 2019, *https://ipolitics.ca/2019/02/25/butts-entitled-to-severance-despite-resigning-from-pmo/*.

279   "Justin Trudeau defends taxpayer-financed nannies," CBC News, Dec. 9, 2015, *https://www.cbc.ca/news/politics/trudeau-defends-nannies-1.3358162*.

on Fogo Island, N.L., surfed in Tofino, hit the beach in the Bahamas, added extra personal time to an official trip to Japan to celebrate an "anniversary" that had actually already passed, and caught Hamilton on Broadway during a getaway to New York City.[280]

Once, when Trudeau had come home from a rare trip doing actual government business in Boston and New York in May 2018, he flew all the way back to Ottawa on the government's private Challenger jet just to pick up Sophie. He waited on the tarmac in the plane for over two hours for her, just to turn around and fly all the way back again to New England, this time for a couples' vacation in Vermont. The entire cost of all that plane time? Almost $12,000.[281] And when he went on a 10-day world tour later that year, he managed — somehow — to rack up a food bill of over $140,000. That's over $14,000 per day. The liquor bill alone for Trudeau and his entourage was over $1,000. But that was peanuts compared to the bill he and his team racked up on their whirlwind tour to Buenos Aires for the G20. The meeting lasted all of two days, but that didn't stop Trudeau and his party pals from spending over $100,000 on food and in-flight expenses, and more than $900 on booze.[282]

And back when Trudeau went to attend a State Dinner at the White House with then president Barack Obama in 2016, he was less concerned about bringing important government officials than he was with loading up the plane with his friends and family. He brought his wife, his mother and his in-laws. But at a time when Canada was trying to get Obama to take his foot off the neck of Canada's oil exports,

---

280   Brian Lilley, "Canada's jet-setting PM Trudeau: One year, ten vacations," Rebel Media, Jan. 3, 2017, *https://www.therebel.media/canada_s_jet_setting_pm_ trudeau_one_year_ten_vacations?page=2.*

281   Sheila Gunn Reid, "Exclusive: Government jet use for Trudeau's romantic getaway to Vermont cost taxpayers nearly $12K," Rebel Media, Jan. 28, 2019, *https:// www.therebel.media/exclusive-government-jet-use-for-trudeau-s-romantic-getaway-to- vermont-cost-taxpayers-nearly-12k.*

282   Sheila Gunn Reid, "Revealed: Trudeau rang up $384K in food, liquor on only five flights," Rebel Media, April 23, 2019, *https://www.therebel.media/justin- trudeau-g20-cost-plane-trips-airbus-food-wine-booze-bill.*

Trudeau just didn't have room to bring Natural Resources Minister Jim Carr.[283]

The Trudeau era has been all about the luxuries of leading, rather than actual leadership. He lectures Canadians about drinking water out of supposedly more environmentally friendly glasses (or "paper-like drink box water bottles sort of things") and makes a show about banning plastics.[284] But records show his family actually spends hundreds of dollars a month on bottled water.[285]

At the prime minister's cottage at Harrington Lake, Trudeau has added a fleet of boats that would make the Canadian Navy jealous. He had taxpayers buy him a ski boat — which on its own would cost tens of thousands of dollars — a pontoon boat (likely about the same), a sailboat, a windsurfer, a 17-foot prospector canoe (specifically in red), one flat water kayak, one river kayak and two stand-up paddleboards.[286] Why couldn't he pay for his own toys himself, like the rest of us do?

But even that wasn't going to be enough luxury summer living for the prime minister, his TV celebrity wife and their team of nannies. He installed a sauna, at taxpayers' expense. They spent nearly $10,000 of taxpayers' money to build an apiary for bees, another $6,000 on an organic garden, plus another $13,500 for a fence around the garden to keep wildlife away. They spent thousands more to improve the ice on the ice-skating rink at the cottage, and still that wasn't enough. They

---

283   John Paul Tasker, "Barack Obama invited Margaret Trudeau to state dinner, prime minister says," CBC News, May 9, 2016, *https://www.cbc.ca/news/politics/margaret-trudeau-state-dinner-1.3573846.*

284   "Trudeau gets tongue-tied when asked how his family is cutting out plastic waste," Daily Hive, June 11, 2019, *https://dailyhive.com/vancouver/justin-trudeau-tongue-tied-cutting-plastic-waste-video.*

285   Sheila Gunn Reid, "Docs reveal: Trudeau spends hundreds on bottled water (after telling you not to buy it)," Rebel Media, Sept. 28, 2017, *https://www.therebel.media/docs_reveal_trudeau_spends_hundreds_on_bottled_water.*

286   Sheila Gunn Reid, "Exclusive: Taxpayers top-up Trudeau's "armada" of Harrington Lake pleasure craft," Rebel Media, Dec. 26, 2018, *https://www.therebel.media/exclusive-taxpayers-top-up-trudeau-s-armada-of-harrington-lake-pleasure-craft.*

evidently also demanded a treehouse with its very own zipline.[287] How does one even possibly manage to make an organic garden cost $6,000? I thought it was just dirt and seeds.

He even apparently pushed to have a helipad installed at Harrington Lake.[288] Maybe he's finding the 30-minute drive from Ottawa is becoming a real pain.

Imagine the spread the Trudeaus have built for themselves on the taxpayers' dime just at that one spot in Harrington Lake. The expensive gardens. The tree house for the kids. The zipline. The fleet of boats. The ice-skating rink. Trudeau even had a sauna put in.[289] And next he wants a helipad. It's the kind of thing regular Canadians can only dream about.

It calls to mind the image of the kind of lake house you might picture from The Godfather II movie, or the beach house that Tony Soprano wanted to buy. It's the kind of opulence fit for a real boss of a real empire. Perhaps the rumours are true — that he's actually letting his mother live there for free, as an added perk.

But the prime minister isn't supposed to be the boss of an empire, let alone a nefarious one. He's supposed to be a public servant. He's the head MP in a Parliament of the people, representing taxpayers and expected to be responsible and accountable and transparent.

Those were the things that Trudeau promised to get elected. But he stabbed Canadians in the back. He stands for none of those things. He lied, cheated, deceived and plundered. He has used his fake compassion,

287   Sheila Gunn-Reid, "Trudeau demands organic garden, apiary, treehouse (with zip line) and more for Harrington Lake residence," Jan. 3, 2019, *https://www. therebel.media/update-trudeau-demands-organic-garden-apiary-tree-house-with-zip-line-and-more-for-harrington-lake-residence*.

288   Brian Lilley "A taxpayer-funded helipad for PM's cottage?" *Toronto Sun*, Jan. 3, 2019, *https://torontosun.com/news/national/lilley-a-taxpayer-funded-helipad-for-trudeaus-cottage*.

289   Sheila Gunn Reid, "Update: Trudeau's $65K sauna saga — Here's what the CBC didn't report," Rebel Media, Jan. 8, 2019, *https://www.therebel.media/update-docs-reveal-real-reason-taxpayers-were-spared-from-trudeau-s-65k-sauna-plans*.

feminism and progressivism to mask a dark, angry, vengeful side. A side that disbelieves inconvenient women when they accuse him or his loyal friends of sexual assault. A side that bullies women of colour when they don't shut up and do what he says. All to get his hands on the levers of power and wealth. So he could reward himself and his cronies. So he could bail his corrupt friends out of trouble. So he could use his office to help dictators and countries that sponsor terror, to enrich Islamic terrorists, and to empower eco-extremists who want to destroy Canada's economy, all so he can enjoy the accolades and advantages given to him by global elites. He'll do anything he must to get anything he can for his own advantage, no matter the damage to Canada, its allies, or patriotic Canadians.

This is no entertaining story like *The Godfather* or *The Sopranos*. This is real life. This is the very real story of one man who has resorted to breaking the law and undermining our economy, our democracy, our values and even our justice system to get everything he wants. This is no movie. This is real life. This is the Libranos.

ABOUT EZRA LEVANT
AND REBEL NEWS

Rebel News's motto is "telling the other side of the story." Founded in Canada in 2015 by Ezra Levant and other journalists from the Sun News Network, we've produced more than 13,000 news videos from four continents, attracting more than 1.25 million YouTube subscribers. We ensure our independence through our unique approach to viewer crowdfunding. Learn more at *RebelNews.com*

Manufactured by Amazon.ca
Bolton, ON

24174549R00077